One Hungry Child

by Carol Dunitz

"In this land of plenty it is a travesty that even one child goes to bed hungry. Hunger and malnutrition are not only the problems of far-away places - we can find them right here in our own communities. We have the knowledge and the resources to end hunger in America; all we need is the will to put them into action. The stories in this volume remind us of the power each of us has to turn the wheels that together can move a nation or a world. By supporting the efforts of the hundreds of local hunger-relief agencies that make up America's Second Harvest, together we can take America past the time when its children knew hunger's misery."

Sen. Patrick Leahy
(D-Vermont)

ONE HUNGRY CHILD

CAROL DUNITZ

Food Bank of Oakland County
Pontiac, MI

Dunitz, Carol
      One Hungry Child / Carol Dunitz.
      p. cm.
ISBN 0-9760330-0-3
1. Hunger—Fiction. 2. Children—Fiction.
I. Title.
All of the characters and events in this book are fictitious, and any resemblance
to actual persons, living or dead, is purely coincidental.
First Edition
10 9 8 7 6 5 4 3 2 1

for more information, please visit
www.OneHungryChild.com

DEDICATION

This book is dedicated to John van Hengel who innovated the concept of food banking in 1967, seventeen years before the Food Bank of Oakland County ever opened its doors.

Table of Contents

FOREWORD

As the President and CEO of America's Second Harvest, The Nation's Food Bank Network, I was very honored and intrigued when I was asked to write the foreword for this book.

Honored - because the stories in this book represent the hundreds of thousands of touching and true ways children's lives are changed thanks to the caring network of food pantries, food banks, and food rescue organizations that cover our great United States.

Intrigued –because the title suggests so much. As long as there is even one hungry child, one starry-eyed infant or growing teen, we as a collective body of caring citizens, have not done enough.

The food banks and rescue organizations depend upon you to help, not passively, but actively; not occasionally but continuously. Are you looking for the "two for one" sales at your local grocery stores? Those extra cans of food could easily be donated to a father or mother who is unemployed.

Have you participated in the National Association of Letter Carrier's Food Drive the second Saturday in May of every year? By simply placing a few boxes or cans of nutritious food in your mailbox, you could help to make the lives of school children much more productive. A hungry child cannot learn.

I've seen benign neglect of the war on poverty and hunger. Apathy, ignorance, confusion, and disbelief are all common barriers to real action. The clicking of tongues at a homeless family will not change the fact that every person in that family, especially the children, deserves a meal that you could provide. Did you know that over 13 million children live in food insecure households?

In the back of this book you will find an envelope. Today, at this very moment--even before you read the ten touching tales between this magnificent cover, slip a check into the envelope and mail it to your local food bank, pantry, or food rescue organization.

Each of us can do something, can't we? Purchasing food, donating food, or generously sharing our wealth, everyone can ensure that in every corner of this marvelous land, there will never be one hungry child.

May my God bless you.

Robert Forney
President and CEO
America's Second Harvest

Introduction

As the Executive Director of a medium-sized food bank operating on a $2.4 million budget, I find myself seeking large bodies of people who might listen to the true stories that I have heard—from people who have faced devastating life altering experiences—about the difference a food providing agency can make in their lives.

My plan is always simple. Find the audience, and spend about 25% of the allotted time addressing hunger facts and food bank statistics. Then, finish the talk with 75% of the time dedicated to the empowering tales from the pantries and soup kitchens we serve.

These stories are so moving that most people open their checkbooks and write a check before I leave the room so that seniors, the "working poor," and children can be helped.

This book was an idea that was birthed after one of those speaking engagements. A woman walked up to me and said, "You should compile some of these stories into a book."

And so I did.

With the help of Dr. Carol Dunitz, a bright and creative artistic type, ten stories from local and national agencies are presented in a simplistic manner. The goal: Encourage the reader to support their favorite hunger relief agency.

Literally.

In the back of the book, following ten beautiful renditions of hunger-themed drawings by young children, you will find a return-envelope. Simply send a check to your favorite pantry, child-oriented agency, or soup kitchen.

And do it now. Please.

For a hungry child, there is no time to ponder, "Should I give or shouldn't I?" A hungry child needs food now.

Robert Forney, President and CEO of America's Second Harvest, has written the foreword. Children have decorated the pages, an illustrator has filled in the blanks with marvelous inked etchings, and we've provided you with an envelope.

All that you have to do now is read the stories and write (the check), that is. It's a simple task but one that will help to feed at least One Hungry Child.

From our table to yours, peace.

Helen Kozlowski-Hicks
Executive Director
Food Bank of Oakland County

ACKNOWLEDGEMENTS

A book like the one you are about to read only
happens when many people come together to participate in its
development. I wish to thank all the people who generously
contributed and directed me to others who could provide story
ideas. They are: Helen Kozlowski-Hicks (*Uncle Bob*); Phyllis
Haynes, Arkansas Food Bank and Anthony Lowrey, Dalton
Whetstone Boys and Girls Club (*Pizza Man*); Rev. Faith
Fowler, Cass Community Social Services (*Mom's Place*); Lea
Luger and Linda Chordash, Yad Ezra (*Powdered Doughnuts*);
Lisa Cain, God's Helping Hands and Don Thomas Asselin,
'Big Brother' for State of Michigan Family Independence
Agency (*Where Are the Potatoes?*); Rev. Barbara Fry, All Saints
Episcopal Church's Bound Together (*Gotcha Days*); Bea
Hanson, Food Bank of Corpus Christi (*Padre Island Dad*);
Linda Linseman, Lighthouse (*Social Security Blues*); Jane
Avery, Community Harvest Food Bank of Northeast Indiana
and Maria Heredia, Southside High School-Fort Wayne (*A
Good Deed Is Never Lost*); and Scott Young, Food Bank of

Lincoln and Sara Fentress, Matt Talbot Kitchen and Outreach (*Mother of the Night*).

I am indebted to Renee Wightman and Helen Kozlowski-Hicks who edited and proofread the stories. Helen also has written a moving introduction. I want to thank Robert Forney, President and CEO of America's Second Harvest, for his meaningful foreword. I would like to extend words of appreciation to Judy Gallegos, who consulted with me on Spanish phrases and Hispanic culture. Thanks, too, to C & B Scene for marketing assistance.

The Food Bank of Oakland County would not have been able to take on this project without the support of its Board of Directors. We appreciate the confidence they have had in the project's success and believe that it will soon be rewarded. Thank you, also, to our friends who have made financial donations to help underwrite some of the expenses involved in mounting a project like this one: Betmar Charitable Foundation; Mr. and Mrs. Herschel P. Blessing; Comerica Bank; Kemp, Klein, Umphrey & Endelman Foundation; Servant Church of St. Alexander; St. Andrew Catholic Church; and St. Daniel Church.

Carol Dunitz, Ph.D.
September 2004

Index of Illustrations

I

UNCLE BOB

✦ ✦ ✦

We are the wealthiest country on earth, and yet we have hungry people still in our richest communities. We encourage businesses to improve and reduce process waste. But this reduces the available food supply for food banks. We need to work as a community to fight the war on hunger.

Vincent G. Dow
Vice President - Distribution Operations
DTE Energy

The minister finished his eulogy. He looked up from his pulpit and surveyed the crowd that had gathered to honor a man they all loved. Rarely had he seen the chapel swollen beyond capacity for a funeral, but today, every pew was filled, every seat was taken. Adults leaned against the interior walls to support themselves during the service when there was no place left to sit. Four young people sat crosslegged on the floor. All were there intent on paying their respects.

Before preparing his remarks, the minister had called on family and close friends to share information with him about the deceased. He had carefully chosen stories to relate during his remarks but felt a twinge of guilt, recognizing his own inability to convey the spirit of the man who now lay in the coffin before them. He was relieved that many of them had volunteered to participate in the service. His eyes met with a portly, sallow-complexioned gentleman in his early 70s who was sitting in the second row. He was bald with a white handlebar mustache. His dark suit was carefully tailored, his shirts custom-made and monogrammed. That morning, his wife had suggested he put on a conventional tie, but he balked. Instead, he had selected his favorite polka-dotted bow tie. He was sure Uncle Bob would have wanted it that way.

He had looked at himself in the mirror as he carefully adjusted it and smiled. For a moment, he saw himself as the youthful vision he had been decades earlier. "What can I say at the funeral," he wondered, "to adequately pay homage to my dear friend? Perhaps," he thought, "it will come to me in the sanctity of the chapel."

He reached for his cane which rested against the side of the pew in which he was seated. Moving out of the pew, he slowly proceeded down the center aisle. As he approached the pulpit, the minister stepped aside to give him access to the microphone.

"Bob and I go back a long way," he commenced. He felt his throat tighten with emotion and he attempted to clear it and proceed. "I could tell you about the saucy pranks we played in college, or the slick deals we made in business, or the trips we took together with our wives. These are special memories for me, but they don't begin to address what a special person Bob was.

He was always thinking of others. He was always trying to figure out how he could help those in need. Mind you, he didn't always approach issues the way most of us do. Sometimes, he would present me with such outrageous ideas; I wondered where they came from. But they were always intended to spread joy and happiness.

"I remember one call he made to me maybe ten years ago or so. 'I've got a great idea,' he told me. 'You know the Baldwin Center? They have some terrific kids participating in their Kids Café Program. And I don't think any of them have ever had their own bike. I told the director I'd deliver 100 new bicycles for the kids. How many will you spring for?'

"He would have paid for all those bikes himself if it had come to that, but he knew his friends would come through. As I see it, he was doing all of his buddies who decided to help a favor. He was giving us an opportunity to give of ourselves. The day those bikes were delivered I think I experienced more pleasure from seeing the expressions on those kids' faces than they did from the new bicycles they were given. Bob truly understood the meaning of 'it's better to give than receive.'"

Having finished his remarks, he bowed his head for a moment. He then reached for his cane and headed back toward his seat to rejoin his wife. As he descended from the pulpit, a handsome young man at the back of the sanctuary strode forward to take his place. He had a sturdy, athletic build and took long, sure-footed strides that suggested more confidence than one might have expected of a young man barely twenty years of age. He had piercing brown eyes, and he had a story to tell.

"I was one of those kids who got a bike," he announced. "Uncle Bob couldn't have possibly known how

much it meant to me. I was eleven years old and it was my first bicycle. It was the most beautiful thing I had ever seen except perhaps for the hotrod some guy down the block was working on. But he couldn't even get his wheels to budge. Me, I whizzed up and down the block on my bike every day like there was no tomorrow. And when I was finished riding, I would carefully bring it in the house where I dusted it and leaned it on its kickstand.

"It was more than a bike. It made me feel like I was someone. It made me feel like I was special. Uncle Bob had a way of doing that. He always made you feel special. He paused but continued shortly. You know where that bike is today? It's in my garage, a constant reminder of the difference a little love and attention can make. I can't bring myself to part with it. Maybe one day, I will have a son who will be able to ride it." He smiled, and then an expression of pain seemed to pass over his face.

"Those of us who attended Baldwin's Children's Programs had a special relationship with one another. We had a hot meal at four in the afternoon every day after school, which would hold you over 'til the next day if you didn't get a good dinner at home. We were tutored on subjects we needed help with. We had the chance to play games and work on art projects. And we all got a bike. It seemed like some kind of miracle at the time. Christmas in the middle of summer, only better than Christmas.

"Then the next day, two of the kids who were in the program with me didn't have their bikes anymore. I worried that mine would disappear, that it was too good to be true, that it was all a dream. We later found out that their dad had taken their bikes down to the pawn shop as soon as they got home. It didn't seem right. I felt real bad for them, and so did Uncle Bob, only he knew that if he gave them both another bike, those bikes would be pawned, too.

"Sometimes, I was jealous of those kids because Uncle Bob gave them special attention. I got to go to summer camp once in a while. But they went up north for a week at Camp Kenowin every summer. One of them wanted a karaoke machine and Uncle Bob bought it for him. Of course, it did stay at the Baldwin Center so we all had the opportunity to use it. I guess Uncle Bob figured his parents would pawn it like the bikes if it were taken home. At the time, I didn't understand why they seemed to get extra attention, but now I know why. Uncle Bob knew they needed it.

"Uncle Bob was everything to us. He made the difference between being a gang member or a happy kid. His giving knew no bounds. I loved the man as much as I loved my family. He was my family. He was my 'Uncle Bob.'"

A buxom white woman with a very round figure approached the pulpit next. The cranberry-colored suit she wore had seen better days, but it was clean and pressed. One might have drawn the conclusion that she had found it at the Clothes Closet at the Baldwin Center. People donated clothing for which they no longer had any use.

Then people who needed clothes could get them at no cost. She looked the other side of fifty, weary but proud. Her face was weathered and her hands were calloused. She was a woman who had clearly spent her life staying only a step or two from poverty, performing countless menial tasks to make ends meet.

"It's not something I like to remind myself of, but now is the time if there ever was one," she commenced. "If you're wondering how low a body can go, you don't want to know. It was more winters ago than I can count. Daddy lost his job. We tried to make ends meet on my pay, but my paycheck alone didn't take us from week to week. When you gotta choose between food and rent, the choice is easy. You gotta eat. And the kids gotta eat. We got thrown out on the street and only knew of one place to go—the Baldwin Center.

"When Uncle Bob heard about it, he arranged for a motel room for us. He paid for that room until Daddy could get back on his feet again. And he sent his wife, Aunt Marge, over with groceries every week. The two of them, they were like angels sent from Heaven. I don't know what would have happened to us without them.

"As bad as it got back then, I did come to understand that there is always someone who has it rougher than you. Uncle Bob and Aunt Marge got my kids involved in a program at the Center. They learned a lot from every experience there. And so did I."

When it became clear that she was finished with her remarks, a young woman halfway back in the sanctuary called out as she rose from her seat. "I remember when Uncle Bob took us all to the circus." She quickly moved past those sitting in her row and out to the center aisle. You could tell she was about to burst with her message but was summoning up all her restraint to stop herself from continuing to speak before she reached the front of the church. She wanted to face everyone as she spoke.

She was neatly groomed and wore a simple shirtwaist dress, not stylish but clean and presentable. She appeared nervous, but not too nervous to declare her admiration for Uncle Bob and testimony for how he had changed her life. Her eyes sparkled as she shared the wonder of the experience.

"Two buses arrived to pick us all up at the Center. I felt lucky because some very kind volunteers rode on my bus. They told us about all the wonderful things we would see there, and promised us kids cotton candy! We arrived early and Uncle Bob had arranged for us to ride an elephant. At first I was scared, but we all tried and when I got up on top of that elephant, I felt like I was on top of the world. Sometimes, you have to push yourself to try to do something you're afraid of. I'll probably never ride an elephant again, but I'll never forget what it felt like to conquer my fear.

"After that field trip, the two buses returned us to the Center. In the past, the buses always left and were taken back to the Rental Center. This time, they remained at the Center permanently. We used them often for other field trips. I didn't know it then, but I later learned that Uncle

Bob bought the buses for us. Imagine that." The young woman returned to her seat as quickly as she had left it.

Next and as it turned out, and last, the former development director from the Baldwin Center approached the pulpit. She was an attractive woman in her early forties who was the first person on the Center staff to come in contact with the man they would all come to know and love as Uncle Bob. Her demeanor was confident. She was dressed in an Anne Klein suit with matching low-heeled shoes. Her shoulder-length hair was lightly brushed and her nails were manicured in a subdued pink shade appropriate for the occasion.

"It seems like yesterday that I spoke with Uncle Bob for the first time, but it is really many yesterdays ago. I did not know him then. He was like any other person at the other end of the line who called the Baldwin Center. Well, perhaps he was more curious than most. He asked me all sorts of questions about the Center, and I attempted to answer them as best I could. I was enthusiastic about my job, and I think I rambled for at least five minutes without coming up for air, at which point he thanked me for the information and hung up.

"I didn't give that conversation another thought until a month later when he called again. I immediately recognized his voice, that of a well-spoken, highly educated man in his late sixties or early seventies. He told me he wanted to take a tour of the facility with his wife, Marge, and their son, Robert. It wasn't something I was asked to arrange very often, but the request was not so unusual that I thought anything special about it. I made the arrangements.

"They arrived at the appointed day and hour. I remember that he was recovering from hip replacement surgery and walked with no pain but some difficulty. She was a striking former model, pencil thin. Their son was a handsome young man in his early twenties. I gave them the tour after which they thanked me and then left without comment. A month passed and Bob called again.

"This time, he invited me out to lunch at a now defunct watering hole, the Birmingham Tavern. In the middle of lunch, he pulled out his checkbook and said he wanted to make a long-term pledge of $50,000 to the Baldwin Center. To tell you I was surprised would be an understatement. I was stunned. While I had mastered some introductory fundraising techniques, I had never been on the receiving end of such a large bequest.

"'Why did you choose us?' I asked, after regaining my composure.

"'Because you took the time to answer my questions when I called you and because you cared,' he replied.

"Over the years, I, too, began to call Uncle Bob and Aunt Marge. They donated a lot of time and money to ensure the Baldwin Center could provide essential services to the children in the Baldwin community. We cared about them and they cared about us."

Upon concluding, she looked over at the minister who had been sitting off to the side. He rose to return to his pulpit to conclude his remarks. Once there, he opened his Bible and recited words from Isaiah 6:8. "Then I heard the voice of the Lord saying, 'Whom shall I send? And who will go for us?' And I said, 'Here am I, send me!'"

✦ ✦ ✦

CHAPTER 2

PIZZA MAN

✦ ✦ ✦

I cannot read these stories and fail to recognize that I am the one that needs to act -- right here, right now -- to give all children, not just the ones who live in my neighborhood, a real chance at life. I can make a difference in something as important as a child's future. Does life offer any greater privilege than that?

Terry A. Barclay
President and CEO
Women's Economic Club &
Women's Leadership Forum

It was one o'clock in the morning. Antoine Edwards was at the end of his shift. After he delivered the last three pizzas on the seat beside him to the address on his assignment sheet, he could go home. He was feeling very tired, after spending most of the day studying for an important final exam and half the night delivering pizzas. He cautiously rode down the urban side street looking for the address on his delivery form.

Antoine slowed his car when he found the address he was looking for and pulled into the driveway. As he stepped out of the car, he thought of the test he had to take the next day and the plans he had with his girlfriend the following evening.

Antoine was driving an old Chevy, which he had been fortunate enough to pick up for only $500 at a local auto auction. The two-tone blue paint was rusted out in many places, and there were some unsightly dents on the side panels that would have made the car aesthetically unacceptable to many. But this didn't bother Antoine. His main objective when purchasing the vehicle was to find a car that was mechanically sound.

On the day of the auction, Antoine had asked one of his cousins who worked as a mechanic at a gas station to come along with him to check the car out and make sure it was in good condition. Once he'd been given the OK, Antoine had made his winning bid. He had smiled widely as he counted out the bills he gave to the owner. He was the proud owner of dependable basic transportation.

Not all of Antoine's friends from high school were making the kinds of choices he had made. One of them, who like Antoine was only twenty-one years old, was tooling around in a current model Mercedes Benz. He always made fun of Antoine and his jalopy. "Start dealin' for me," he often coaxed Antoine, "and you can be driving one of these." Antoine always ignored the offer. His friend had made decisions that were taking him in a very different direction. Antoine had no intention of getting caught up in drugs.

Antoine was finishing his last semester at community college. He'd been delivering pizzas for three years to earn money to put himself through school. He was very excited about earning his associate's degree at the end of the month and had received a scholarship from the state university. He was a young man with a very bright future.

Antoine turned around and reached for the insulated hot bag, which held the three remaining pizzas. He grabbed the bag in both hands and pulled it toward him. As he stood up, he felt someone grab him from behind, wrenching his arms behind him. In the process, he let the hot bag drop to the ground. "Get his wallet," he heard his assailant tell an accomplice.

"It's in the car," Antoine volunteered, trying to cooperate.

"Who asked you?" The second man's voice almost sounded like that of a boy, not a man. It had a harsh edge to it.

Antoine stood motionless under the tight grip of the man who had spoken first. He watched silently as the other one rustled around in his car looking for the wallet. When the young man emerged from the car, he held up the wallet triumphantly.

"Now get the pizzas," the first man reminded his partner.

"I got 'em." His eyes met Antoine's as he grabbed the hot bag. "But I think this guy could squeal on me if he saw me in a lineup," he answered.

"Then you know what to do," the other responded.

"I don't think I can do that, Martin."

"What'd you say my name for, dummy? Now you gotta do it."

Antoine felt a sharp blade pierce his skin and enter his chest. He grabbed where the pain was as he fell to the pavement. There was blood oozing from the wound. He seemed vaguely aware that the two hoodlums had run off and thought to cry out but knew that in the silence of the night, nobody would hear him. With his free arm, he struggled to pull his cell phone from his jacket pocket. He dialed 9-1-1 and felt tears in his eyes when he heard the female voice at the other end. He tried to call out but heard only faint sounds emanate from his mouth. He desperately hoped that someone would find him.

✦ ✦ ✦

"There's never anything *good* to eat in this house," fifteen year-old Bobby Porter complained.

"There's never anything to eat in this house," his nineteen year-old brother Martin corrected him. "Call and order some pizza for us, Jovan," Martin demanded, looking his younger brother squarely in the eyes.

"You ain't got the money for pizza," Jovan responded.

"So what?" Martin answered. "You just have it sent down the street to one of the neighbor's houses. Me and Bobby gonna take care of the rest."

"I won't do that," Jovan responded.

"You don't like pizza?" Martin taunted him.

"You know I like pizza," Jovan responded.

"Then just do what I tell you, little brother."

"I don't like the way you're planning to pay for the pizza," Jovan returned, cowering as he spoke.

"And what would that be?" Martin asked menacingly. "You been snoopin' where you shouldn't be snoopin'?"

Jovan did not respond. There was something about Martin that sometimes frightened him. Martin passed him a sheet of paper with a phone number and address handwritten on it. "Call that number and have three pizzas delivered to the address I wrote down. Order any toppings you want, little bro," he told him cavalierly. "It's on me," he added, laughing with mock generosity.

Jovan looked at the sheet of paper. He didn't want to make the call but he also didn't want to be the butt of Martin's anger. He did what his brother asked him.

An hour later, he, Martin, Bobby and a few of their friends were sitting around, partying while their younger sisters and brothers looked on. They stuffed themselves with the three large pizzas, which had more toppings than Jovan had ever even dared to fantasize about in his dreams. Martin and Bobby were heroes.

Jovan remembered the last time he and his mother had a falling out. It had happened several months earlier. His mother had entered the back bedroom where he had been soundly asleep. It was just past noon.

"What time are you gonna sleep to anyway?" his mother chided him in a demanding tone. "You just a lazy thang like your older brothers. You don't watch it," she warned, "and you gonna land in jail just like them." She tugged at one of the shades and it snapped back to its rod.

Daylight filled the room confirming his mother's announcement that he was wasting the day away. He hid his head under his pillow trying to block out the sun's rays, as well as the foreboding picture his mother painted of his future.

It had been three years since Martin was sent away to prison for killing a young man delivering pizzas. He hadn't

actually knifed the guy. Bobby had done that. But he had
held him and ordered Bobby to do the dirty work. Bobby
had just followed his orders much the way Jovan had when
Martin had demanded he order the pizzas. Of course, Jovan
had no idea at the time that Martin and Bobby would kill
someone. Nonetheless, he still felt a twinge of guilt for
having a small part in the affair.

When Jovan thought about Martin, he figured his
brother could count on being in prison for a long time. He
probably wouldn't have to serve the whole sentence, so it
would be something less than a lifetime—but that was
hardly consolation. And Bobby wasn't any better off. Sure,
he'd gotten off easy the first time because he had been a
juvenile, but just last year, he'd gunned down some kid who
was trying to hijack his car. Jovan had to concede the law
didn't look favorably on people who went around killing
other people, even if they thought it was justified. Bobby
had been put away, too.

"That's right," his mother reiterated. "You gonna
spend the better part of your life behind bars just like your
good-for-nothin' brothers." Jovan's mother knew that he
belonged to a gang just as his brothers had, but she didn't
know what to do about it. Sometimes, he'd come home from
fistfights in such a state she wondered if he'd recover. She
wanted to help her son, but the only way she knew was to
challenge his activities and that just seemed to increase his
resolve to make the same kinds of mistakes his brothers had.

Jovan jumped out of bed. At sixteen, he was tall and lean, and towered over his mother. He drew his arm up in the air as if to take a swing at her. "I had it," he told her. "Always goin' on, blabbin' at the mouth. You don't understand nuthin."

"Don't you raise a hand to me," she started back at him. "I knowed enough not to get in trouble with the law. I knowed enough not to get involved with a bunch o' no-good roughnecks. I knowed enough to…." She felt the pain of his palm against her face. "OK, you gone and done it now. Out of my house, and I don't want to see you back here ever again. You done crossed the line, Jovan. I don't want to have any part of you." She turned away from him because she didn't want him to see the pain in her eyes. The slap was nothing compared to the fresh acceptance that another one of her sons was most certainly taking the wrong path.

Jovan had been cocky about the whole episode. He figured he could stay with some of his friends, but things didn't work out the way he planned. Some of his friends' parents let him stay with them for a few days. In one case, he was put up for a week, but it wasn't too long before he no longer had anywhere to go. It had been difficult to accept that just like him, his tough friends remained dependent on their parents, only they weren't so foolish as he'd been to challenge their authority.

That's when Jovan called his Auntie Maddie. Maddie was his mother's older sister. Unlike his mother who had eight children, Maddie was childless. She had never experienced either the joy or tribulations associated with having children, so when Jovan called she was open to having him come and stay with her.

Maddie was, he discovered, aware of what had transpired between him and his mother, and had strict rules she expected to him follow. To say that Jovan wasn't excited about this would be an understatement. He'd followed his own rules only for as long as he could remember. But he liked his Auntie Maddie, and he thought he'd try things her way. He'd learned since he left his mother's a few weeks earlier that there was more to being an adult than calling yourself one.

Jovan's attitude improved while staying with Auntie Maddie. She claimed it had nothing to do with living with her. "It happened," she said, "because he was ready." While living with Auntie Maddie, Jovan could have hung out with his old buddies or joined one of the gangs in her neighborhood, but he didn't.

At her suggestion, he got involved in a Youth Enrichment Program at the Boys and Girls Club near her. The coordinator, Brother Ron, took a liking to him and was always there to talk with him when something was on his mind. Brother Ron wasn't quite old enough to be his dad, but he did fit the role of a father figure offering guidance and support.

In the afternoon after school, Jovan would often lift weights or pick up a game of basketball with some of the other guys. He even worked at the club a few hours a week to get spending money. When he managed to make more than he spent, he would give it to Brother Ron to put away someplace safe. Eventually, Brother Ron took him to the bank and helped him fill out the forms to establish his own savings account.

Brother Ron was always planting seeds. When he noticed Jovan reading, he decided the time was right to tell him about scholarships that were available for college through the generosity of several donors. Jovan said nothing, but Brother Ron had planted a seed. Over time, Brother Ron noticed Jovan studying after school before he started playing ball.

When Jovan turned seventeen, he announced to Aunt Maddie that he intended to go to college. "That's a fine ambition," she told him, delighted that he had set a positive goal for himself, though she questioned his resolve. No one in the family had ever gone to college, and the idea seemed unattainable. When he brought home his year-end report card barely a month later, she recognized he was serious. He had all A's and B's.

Over the summer, Jovan took a computer class in a special program at the local community college for high school students. He had come full circle. Unlike his older brothers, he managed to get through the difficult stage when the wrong friends can do great damage. He was happy and productive, and a wonderful role model for his younger brothers and sisters who, along with his mother, he now saw often.

Jovan applied at a local pizza shop and was given the afternoon shift delivering pizzas over the summer. Auntie Maddie was so proud of him she told him he could use her car. He worked hard five nights a week.

✦ ✦ ✦

Jovan Porter was at the end of his shift. After he delivered the last pizzas on the seat beside him to the address on his assignment sheet, he could go home. He was feeling very tired after spending most of the day studying for his computer class and half the night delivering pizzas. He cautiously rode down the urban side street looking for the address on his delivery form. He slowed his car when he saw the address he was looking for and pulled into the driveway.

Before he stepped out of the car, he looked around cautiously. He knew there were others out there who were not as fortunate as he was and were still trying to find their way. He carefully stepped out of the car while thinking about the test he had the next day and the plans he had with his girlfriend, Julie. Life was full of promise.

✦ ✦ ✦

CHAPTER 3

MOM'S PLACE

✦ ✦ ✦

Marriage-partner criteria: Good sense of humor, bathes regularly, works hard, helps to feed hungry children. Sorry – I really can't compromise on any of these!

Sharon Lee Remington
Editor & Writer
Detroit, MI

The apartment was dark, as one would have expected at midnight. The tall, wooden windows with splintered jambs had not been caulked in many years and let in more cold air than was acceptable. Unfortunately, the family that lived there could not afford to do anything about it, and the landlord had no intention of correcting the situation. The mother and her eldest son had simply draped old sheets over the windows to supply a modicum of privacy.

The original oak flooring was scratched and worn, having lost its fine veneer during a bygone era. Ten-foot ceilings suggested the building had been erected many decades earlier when labor costs were low and materials were cheap—a time when the need for energy efficiency was unknown. The paint on the wall was peeling.

"Mama. Mama," Luis, who had just turned four, tugged at his mother's nightgown.

"Go back to sleep, Luis," his mother told him in a voice that was half awake, half still in slumber. She had had to work late the night before and did not want to be disturbed from her rest before the alarm clock rang.

"But, Mama, I'm cold. I can't go back to sleep."

Gabriela Gutierrez rolled over and reached for the lamp beside her bed. She pulled the chain once and then once more but the lamp did not illuminate. "Darn bulb has burned out again," she mumbled under her breath. She looked up and saw the shadow of Luis who had now been joined by his twin brother, Tomas.

"Mama, I'm cold," Tomas echoed his brother's words. "It's too cold. Please turn up the heat."

From the back room, Gabriela could hear the baby crying. She threw her covers aside and slowly brought herself to a seated position. The baby had stopped waking her in the middle of the night several months earlier. Gabriela wondered what was the matter. She pulled herself out of bed and stood up. Her long flannel nightgown almost reached to the floor, but her feet were bare and she felt a slight chill herself. She made her way in the dark to her daughter's crib.

"There, there, sweetheart," she told the baby as she picked her up in her arms. "It's OK." She slid a couple of fingers into the baby's diaper to see if it was wet, but curiously, it wasn't wet, it wasn't even damp. She wondered if the baby was crying because she, too, was cold. "It's OK," she repeated, consoling the infant and the two little boys.

But it was not OK.

Gabriela and her five children, ages eighteen months through thirteen years, lived in an old apartment building in the inner city. The building had once been a showplace with all the accoutrements those with more money expect. Over the years, tenants had allowed the urban sprawl to draw them out to the suburbs where they chose more desirable locations with attractive homes.

The building was sold and the new owner catered to those who had a diminished capacity to pay rent. Maintenance was sloppy and the building deteriorated. Still, tenants rushed in because the rooms were spacious, the building was close to stores and a bus stop, and most importantly, the rent was affordable.

Gabriela stood there trying to decide what to do next. The baby was beginning to quiet down, soothed by the warmth of her mother's body. Luis and Tomas were still complaining. Not wanting to wake the other two children, Gabriela fumbled though the dark to the kitchen to get a bottle for the infant. She opened the refrigerator door and was surprised when the light did not come on. She flicked the light switch on the kitchen wall and nothing happened. She started frantically running from light switch to light switch, trying to illuminate any room in the apartment. None of them worked.

"Do you know where the flashlight is?" she asked her two frightened little sons, remembering she had recently seen them playing with it.

"Yes, Mama," Luis and Tomas answered almost in unison.

"Get it, and bring it to me." Her voice was strong and confident, giving them the impression that she had the situation under control. Seconds later, they joined her by the thermostat and handed the flashlight to her. Gabriela turned it on and held it up to see what the temperature of the room was. She always kept the thermostat at sixty-eight degrees, but it only registered fifty-nine degrees.

She wanted to curse the landlord but she did not want to set a bad example. Gabriela suppressed an urge to cry because she did not want to upset her children. She had paid her rent on time just like she did every month. She wondered what she could do now.

"Don't worry," she told the boys, trying to sound cheerful like it was all a game. "Let's all climb into my bed to keep cozy and warm, and we'll fix this problem in the morning." Luis and Tomas rushed over to their mother's double bed, jumped in and snuggled together under the covers.

She took the baby back to the kitchen with her, where she filled a bottle with cold milk. Gabriela wished she could have warmed it up but figured a cold bottle was better than no bottle at all. She returned to her bed with the baby and quickly fell back to sleep.

✦ ✦ ✦

When Gabriela woke up the next morning, the reality of the situation hit her. The landlord had taken her money, which she paid monthly in good faith, and had not only failed to keep the apartment in good repair but had also neglected to pay the utilities. She had resigned herself long ago to living in an apartment with chipped paint and roaches because she didn't have the money for a better place. Now even that possibility was gone. She realized she and her family would have to move, but she had no idea where they could go.

Gabriela and the children hurriedly dressed to protect themselves from the cold. They all ate dry cereal for breakfast. Miguel, Gabriela's thirteen-year-old son and Susana, her nine-year-old daughter, refused milk with their cereal, insisting that they didn't like it.

"Don't worry," she told Miguel and Susana as they left for their respective schools, which were walking distance from the apartment. "I'll get everything taken care of," she reassured them, not knowing how she could possibly accomplish what she promised.

She called her employer before she left to drop off the twins at preschool and the baby at the daycare facility there. "I won't be able to come in today." She explained her predicament and he gave her the day off. Gabriela sighed as she put the phone receiver down. She needed the money, but she needed a suitable place for her family to live even more.

✦ ✦ ✦

Cass Community Social Services is headquartered in the Scott Building just north of downtown Detroit. In operation since the Great Depression, it offers a menu of services including shelter for the homeless, food for the hungry, and assistance for seniors and the mentally challenged. After consulting with some of her friends, Gabriela decided to go over to the Scott Building and look for help. She went with hope but was at the same time worried.

She knew that Cass operated a temporary residential facility, but she also knew most residential facilities insisted that boys over the age of twelve be separated from their families and placed in other settings. She could not bear to have Miguel separated from the rest of the family even if it were only for a short time. She climbed the steps to the front entrance knowing she had no choice. She needed help.

The social worker, Pat, at the Scott Building listened empathically to Gabriela's story, which was not unusual to her. She had helped many single mothers in the past who had similar situations to overcome. The social worker suggested a temporary move to Mom's Place, a residential shelter that keeps families together. Unlike other homeless shelters that will not accept teenage boys, Mom's Place welcomed the whole family.

That evening, the director at Mom's Place welcomed Gabriela and her children. She took time to put everyone at ease. Miguel and Susana appeared to be healthy, but she wondered about their younger siblings. Luis and Tomas complained about how hungry they were. The director wondered if they were suffering from malnutrition and dehydration. The twins looked awfully thin and their eyes appeared to be sunken. She thought their lips looked very dry, too. She knew that younger children, often unintentionally, did not get their fair share of food and drink when there wasn't enough to feed everyone adequately. The director made sure the entire family was well fed at dinner. After giving them extra helpings of chicken and vegetables, she scheduled appointments for them the next day with Dr. Lynn.

Dr. Lynn is the physician at Cass Community Social Services. She generously volunteers her time there three days a week. The center also has a paid nurse practitioner on staff who works part time. These medical professionals enable Cass to offer badly needed healthcare services to their clients.

Dr. Lynn sat forward at the desk in her office, ready to review medical histories with Gabriela Gutierrez. "Let's talk about what's been going on with the children," she suggested.

"It's been a stretch for me," Gabriela told her. "I've been working as a waitress for quite a while now. I am thankful to have the job, but it's long hours and not enough money for the time I put in. There's nothing else I'm prepared to do," she conceded. "I don't get to spend enough time with the children and I have to depend on Miguel to take care of the little ones when I'm not there."

"I imagine he's not too happy about that," the doctor commented.

"Yes, that's right. He resents it," Gabriela agreed.

"But he understands I have to have his help. Otherwise, I don't know what would happen."

"Outside of the financial stresses, Mrs. Gutierrez, how do you think the children are doing?"

"I think that Miguel and Susana are doing real good," she reported. "The others, I'm not so sure. I'm particularly worried about Luis. He doesn't seem to be himself lately."

"What have you observed?" Dr. Lynn asked.

"He has a lot of headaches and he's cranky so much of the time," Gabriela responded.

When their discussion was over, Dr. Lynn gave Gabriela and each of the children comprehensive physical examinations. Just as Gabriela noted, she, Miguel, and Susana were doing well. The younger children, however, were suffering from dehydration because they weren't getting enough liquids. They were also malnourished since their diet lacked the fruits and vegetables they needed. Dr. Lynn figured this was due in part to the cost of these things, but she also recognized that without Gabriela around at mealtimes, Miguel and Susanna probably ate most of what was available without realizing that their younger brothers and sister were not getting enough to meet their needs. The doctor knew that these were all situations that could be turned around at Mom's Place.

Dr. Lynn was, however, especially concerned when she discovered Luis had elevated levels of lead in his blood. The doctor knew that lead poisoning was not uncommon with small children who could get it from deteriorating paint, contaminated household dust, or bare soil outside the house where they played. She hoped his condition was recent and could be reversed. Lead poisoning, left untreated in children under the age of six, could result in reduced IQ, learning disabilities, Attention Deficit Disorder, kidney damage and a host of other irreversible conditions. As it turned out, Luis' problem was observed and treated in time to avoid any complications.

Gabriela and her children lived at Mom's Place for four months. They had a safe, clean, secure home there, where food was plentiful. There was childcare on site and transportation to get them to the places they needed to go. The staff worked with Gabriela to reopen her Family Independence Agency case, and by the time she and her family left Mom's Place, she had a bridge card to help her with the monthly food bill. At the same time, she was given training that enabled her to enter the workforce with badly needed skills, which helped her get a better job. The Gutierrez family got a new start on life at Mom's Place.

✦ ✦ ✦

The receptionist opened the door to the doctor's office. A little boy peeked in, holding the edge of the door with both hands. He looked up at the doctor who was wearing a white lab coat and noticed the stethoscope she had slung around her neck. It was just like on TV except he knew and liked her. Luis waited for her eyes to meet his. He smiled widely when they did. Though most of his face was hidden behind the door, the doctor recognized him immediately though she had not seen him in several months. She knew he was smiling by the twinkle in his eyes.

"C'mon in, Luis," she warmly welcomed him.

Luis skirted out from behind the door and dashed into the room. At the end of his short sprint, he raised his right leg up and using all the momentum he had gained, propelled himself onto the examining table. Luis sat there proudly. He knew there were very few four-year-olds who could accomplish that feat.

"You look terrific," Dr. Lynn told him. She remembered the condition he had been in when she first examined him months earlier and observed a dramatic improvement in his health.

"Yeah," he responded. "I'm drinking eight glasses of water a day like you told me.

"I bet you're peeing a lot more than you used to," Dr. Lynn commented.

"Yeah, I am.

"Glad to hear it. Looks like you put on a little weight, too," Dr. Lynn countered, looking pleased.

"And it's all muscle," Luis bragged, flexing his left arm muscle and showing it off to her.

"Very impressive," the doctor answered, appearing impressed.

"It's all those healthy meals I'm eating, but I still like to have potato chips and chocolate bars sometimes," he confided.

Dr. Lynn smiled. "Anything else you want to tell me about before we start the exam?"

"Some of the other guys at preschool have dirt under their fingernails but not me." Luis stretched his arms out in front of himself with his hands extended, fingers apart. "I always wash my hands after I come in from playing outside. I'm not gonna get that lead poisoning thing again," he told her, demonstrating how responsible he was.

"I don't think you have to worry about it where you're living," Dr. Lynn told him.

"Maybe you're right. I'm living at a different Mom's Place now," he said, grinning from ear to ear, "my Mom's. It's real nice where we live, but I'm not taking any chances."

CHAPTER

4

POWDERED DOUGHNUTS

✦ ✦ ✦

Any civilization that does not provide basic food, medical care, clothing and housing for its children, elderly, and the infirmed cannot call itself truly civilized. This is not a political, geopolitical, religious or social issue. It is not an issue at all. It is a moral imperative and the basis of our humanity.

Howard L. Zoller, Esquire
Oakland County attorney

Once a month, Isaac Fine and his mother visited Yad Ezra, the only Jewish food pantry in metropolitan Detroit. They arrived in an old, grey Dodge that had seen better days, parked in the agency lot at the rear of the building and came in through the back entrance to receive their monthly food allotment.

It was a trip on which his mother counted to make sure she and her son had enough food to carry them through the next four and a half weeks. It was a ritual Isaac looked forward to with glee. He liked walking along the conveyor belt, choosing his favorite sugared cereal and hoping that powdered donuts would be available. He always expected Robin would be there. She was the volunteer he liked best, because she always gave him a lollipop before he and his mother left.

✦ ✦ ✦

Rosalyn Weiss was a depression baby. Born in 1935, she was too young to have actually understood the hardships that were commonplace during that decade. No one in her family had to stand in bread lines or frequent soup kitchens. Her father managed to keep his market going and her mother struggled to make ends meet in an era when customers had little disposable income and by necessity, made do with less. Rosalyn always had enough to eat, even if special foods were only served on Shabbat. Unlike some of the other children she knew, she could depend on a change of clean clothes to wear to school every day. And there was never any worry about losing the family home.

No matter how little there was to go around, there was always a place at their dinner table for those who had less, especially on Shabbat, the day of rest. It was a mitzvah, a good deed, to share with others. Rosalyn remembered her mother saying more than once, "There but for the grace of God go I." She never gave it much thought. Perhaps she had been too young to truly understand the words, but she did grasp their meaning.

Her mother kept a tzedakah box on the kitchen table. She and her father always put spare change in the box and when it was full, it was turned in at Jewish Welfare Federation. Federation used contributions to help those who were less fortunate. After turning in the full tzedakah box, her mother would get an empty one to bring home to fill, and the ritual would start all over again.

When Rosalyn was little, her grandfathers would sometimes give her a few pennies to purchase candy or some other little treat. She especially loved the bright shiny new pennies and would rush to her parents to show them off. As she grew older and times became better, they gave her nickels, dimes or quarters, and sometimes even a dollar bill. Rosalyn always felt privileged to be able to put some of the money her grandparents gave her in the tzedakah box. Even though she was little, it made her feel like she was doing something of great importance. It made her feel very grown up.

In the mid- to late forties, Rosalyn worked at the family grocery store after school and on weekends. As a youngster, she would help place stock on the wooden shop shelves. Sometimes she would shelve cereal boxes or canned goods. Other times she would work in produce. As she grew older, she was allowed to work the cash register, which she really enjoyed because it gave her the opportunity to get to know everyone in the neighborhood. Like everyone else, she came to appreciate the prosperity the war years brought. When people in other parts of the world thought about America, they dreamed of streets 'paved with gold.' Times weren't that good, but almost.

Rosalyn graduated from high school in 1953. Her parents beamed at commencement. Their adorable, five-foot-tall daughter and only child was graduating with honors from Central High School and headed to college in the fall. It was the fulfillment of a dream their parents had had when they escaped the Ukraine years earlier. Their

family would no longer have to live in terror of pogroms—
not knowing when the next organized massacre of Jews
would threaten their lives and the lives of their loved ones.
Their children and their children's children would have
opportunities open to them that had never been possible for
Jews under the Tsar.

✦ ✦ ✦

Years earlier, Rosalyn's maternal grandmother had
cried as their ship approached the New York harbor. The
grand statue of the lady holding the torch seemed to call out
to her. She did not know that engraved at its base were the
words of another Jewish woman, Emma Lazarus, poignantly
welcoming shiploads of people filled with hope, searching for
a better life: "Give me your tired, your poor, Your huddled
masses yearning to breathe free, The wretched refuse of your
teeming shore, Send these, the homeless, tempest-tossed to
me: I lift my lamp beside the golden door."

Rosalyn's grandmother believed like hundreds of
thousands of other Jews who entered the United States through
Ellis Island from the 1880s through the 1920s that America was
truly the land of promise. And she had been right.

Her husband, Avrom, had been a tailor in the
old country. He had always been proud of his work,
meticulously completing every job he had. Many admired
his perfect stitches and the way he could always shape a
garment to flatter the figure of the person who was to wear
it. It was a trade he knew he could continue to practice once

he and his family were settled in Detroit. With a little good fortune, he even hoped to open his own shop. He started taking in work from area cleaners and soon had his own business. He was a resourceful man. And he was a good man who was honest and fair, always thinking of others.

✦ ✦ ✦

Rosalyn fell in love during her junior year of college. Lester Fine was a year older. He was a shy, soft-spoken young man, lanky and tall, almost a foot taller than she was. He was also known as 'an egghead' whose nose was always buried in books. While he didn't play sports like many other young men she knew, or have a multitude of outside interests, Lester worshipped Rosalyn. You could see how much he loved her by the expression on his face and the light in his eyes when he looked at her. She, too, was smitten.

Lester was studying to be an accountant. Rosalyn planned on becoming an elementary school teacher. They were both serious students and decided it was best to finish their studies at the university before getting married.

Her parents planned a lovely summer wedding to which all their family and friends were invited. The wedding was traditional, and after the Rabbi pronounced them 'man and wife,' Lester ceremoniously stomped on the crystal glass wrapped in a napkin, which had been placed at his feet. The sound of the glass shattering resounded throughout the room and everyone cried out, "L'Chaim," which meant "To Life."

Lester took his bride in his arms. He kissed her passionately and then they spent the rest of the evening celebrating with all the guests. It was a warm, joyous wedding, 'belle botische' those who still spoke some Yiddish would say, followed by a honeymoon in Niagara Falls, Canada.

Upon their return, they settled down into a modest apartment for several years and worked hard to save enough money to put a down payment on a small home. Rosalyn and Lester were happy. Life was good. They were, after all, living the American Dream. Only one thing wasn't perfect: they wanted to start a family, but Rosalyn did not become pregnant.

Close to fifteen years passed. Rosalyn and Lester hoped and prayed they would be blessed with a child, but no child was forthcoming. They had long ago accepted the fact that theirs would be a marriage with no children, when Rosalyn went to her doctor complaining of nausea and heartburn only to be informed that she had conceived. She thought of her studies at religious school when she was a youngster. In the Bible, Sarah had given Abraham a child when she was past the age when a woman could expect to bear children. When a stranger visited Abraham and Sarah's tent and said Sarah would have a child, she had laughed much the same way Rosalyn laughed when the doctor had told her she was pregnant.

Rosalyn and Lester looked forward to the baby's arrival with great anticipation. They painted the bedroom adjacent to theirs yellow, since they didn't know if they were to be blessed with a boy or girl. They put up yellow curtains with white trim and hung prints on the walls of children at play. They bought a new dresser and matching crib above which they suspended a colorful mobile. Often Rosalyn would stop on her way home from school to pick out new toys and accessories for the baby who would soon turn their lives upside down.

They spent hours talking about how their lives were about to be transformed. Together, they decided that Rosalyn would quit her job and stay home with the baby. They didn't need the money, and they wanted the child for whom they had been waiting so long to have every possible opportunity.

They combed through baby books trying to figure out what to name their baby, always laughing as they let different names role off their tongues. Finally, they decided that if they had a son, like Abraham and Sarah, they would name him Isaac. Isaac means laughter and they always smiled and laughed when they talked about their new baby. If they had a daughter, they would name her Rachel.

Isaac Fine was born on a perfect summer day. He weighed 7 lbs., 6 oz., was 21 inches long, and as his father remarked immediately upon seeing him, "He has ten fingers and ten toes." He was a handsome baby who sprang from his mother's womb screaming before the obstetrician ever spanked his bottom. He took to nursing immediately, slept for five-hour stretches before he was two months old, and generally turned the Fine household from a sedate sanctuary to a bustling nursery. He was everything for which Lester and Rosalyn had hoped.

But as months passed, Isaac didn't seem to be developing the way his parents expected. Often, he seemed overly quiet, and his eyes didn't seem to focus on them when they stood above his crib. He was unusually slow to respond when they played with him.

At first, Rosalyn thought he was just quiet like his father, but over time she became concerned when she saw how her friends' infants behaved. On a visit to the pediatrician's office, Rosalyn expressed her concern. The doctor ran some tests and then shared the results with Isaac's parents. Isaac was developmentally disabled. He would physically grow into manhood, but he would never have the intellectual capacity of an adult. At best, he might be expected to function at the level of an eight year old.

Another couple might have been devastated by the news they received, but not Rosalyn and Lester. They loved each other deeply and so, too, their son. They showered him with attention and did everything they could to help him achieve within his limitations. He grew and with their help came into his own.

Rosalyn, who was not working outside the home, spent countless hours with him, lovingly teaching him much like she had done with her elementary school students years earlier. Isaac enjoyed helping his parents and was involved in outside programs in which his parents enrolled him. The Fine household was not a typical one, but it was a happy one that provided a nurturing environment for Isaac.

When Lester died suddenly from a heart attack in the late eighties, Rosalyn was faced with a daunting dilemma. She had been out of the workforce for almost twenty years and the prospect of going back to teaching seemed dismal. With a master's degree, nine years of experience in elementary education, and an extended absence from the workplace, it would be difficult to find a job in a marketplace that was cluttered with younger candidates who could work for less. Besides, Isaac needed her.

Once she was able to settle her husband's estate, it appeared that she and her son could manage if she simply took on a substitute teaching position a couple days a week. That is what she did. "It is easy to have twenty-twenty hindsight," she thought to herself years later as she lay immobile in bed, plagued with diabetes and debilitating symptoms associated with it. "I should have put Isaac in a day program and found a full-time job when Lester died, but who knew?" she told the volunteer at Yad Ezra when she first applied for assistance in 1998. "I own my home, but I can't afford to keep food on the table."

✦ ✦ ✦

The Yad Ezra volunteer looked out the window and saw a young man barely out of his teens helping a short, elderly woman out of an old, grey Dodge. He closed the door behind her and took her free arm in his own. With her other arm, the woman held a cane, which she used to help support herself as she painfully limped to the building.

As they came closer, Robin recognized the couple. It was Rosalyn Fine who was close to seventy now and the young man, ah yes, that was her son. He barely looked eighteen because he had lived the stress-free life of an eight-year-old. He was a great help to his mother at home, vacuuming, taking out the garbage and performing other chores. He had the presence recently to call 9-1-1 when his mother fell at home, broke her leg, and couldn't get up.

They entered the building and took seats in the waiting room. Sometimes, there weren't many people waiting. Today, it was busy. Rosalyn asked Isaac to take a number to secure their place in line. When he returned, he sat down beside her.

"Do you think Robin is here today?" he asked his mother, hoping her answer would be "Yes."

"I don't know," Rosalyn answered.

"Do you think they'll have powdered donuts today?" he asked, wanting to be assured that the trip to Yad Ezra would be worthwhile.

"I don't know," Rosalyn hesitated, "but I think they will have something special for you." She smiled at him as she spoke.

"How do you know?" Isaac asked.

"Because this is a special place, Isaac. It's a special place where they go out of their way to help special people like you and me."

Isaac accepted his mother's explanation without question. He pulled a small toy out of his pocket and started to play with it to pass the time. He was slouched in his chair engrossed in child's play when Robin came out to greet him and his mother. And she had a powdered donut and an armful of love.

✦ ✦ ✦

WHERE ARE THE POTATOES?

✦ ✦ ✦

When we neglect to feed the children of our community, we neglect to nourish our community's future and eventually there will be no community.

Augie Fernandes
President and CEO
Gleaners Community Food Bank

Marsha Willis peeked out from the office area. It was a busy day at the pantry known as God's Helping Hands. More people were there for their monthly food allotment than usual, which meant significantly more work for her and the volunteers. While clients took numbers when they arrived to ensure the food agency's processes moved smoothly, Marsha periodically checked the waiting room to make sure no one was being overlooked.

Every time she surveyed the waiting room that morning, she saw an attractive, well-groomed man sitting in the back of the holding area. She guessed he was probably in his late thirties. He was dressed casually in a light blue polo shirt and khaki pants; his black shoes were shined and looked new. The man's hair was recently styled and he wore it combed back from his face. The visitor was engrossed in a copy of *The New York Times*. He appeared to be an unlikely candidate for her food agency's services.

✦ ✦ ✦

Luke Simms lived alone in a modest neighborhood in Pontiac, Michigan. He had a good job working for the county of Oakland and over the years had managed to save enough money to buy his own home. Luke had been so excited when he signed the papers at the closing. He had dreams of completing many projects around the house, but once he settled in, it was his love of gardening that led him to devote most of his spare time to the quarter-acre lot on which his modest bungalow was situated.

Every winter he longed for the first signs of spring in anticipation of the planting season. He watched attentively in February as the hours of daylight increased. He listened for signs that warm weather was around the corner and was rewarded by the sounds of robins and bluebirds actively preparing for the coming season. He was ecstatic by March, when the crocus shoots began to peek through the earth.

The first summer in his new home, Luke designed a vertical garden on trellises. He planted all sorts of annual flowering vines, each with its own distinct flower. There were faithful scarlet runner beans with their exceptional cardinal color flowers about the size of a quarter, dolichos lablab with its large purple flowers, and many varieties of Morning Glory with four to five petal blossoms that had a silky texture and looked like small saucepans.

He also installed sweet peas, which had a shorter twining vine with delicate flower petals. Sometimes, he would dedicate a trellis to one variety of vine alone. Other times, he would mix the vines that climbed a trellis for a full, wild look. The vines and flowers were his palette. His yard was his canvas.

The second year, he made a pumpkin patch inside the trellised area. The third year, he added a border of extra tall sunflower plants, which reached eight feet at maturity. Under them, he planted bushy flowering nasturtiums with orange, yellow and white blossoms to complement the flowers that towered high above them and bowed their heads to the sun.

His backyard had a spectacular array of colors and textures. Luke would sometimes bring a lawn chair out and sit and admire the manifestation of nature in his yard. It was, he thought to himself, one of God's miracles.

If there was anything Luke enjoyed more than gardening, it was children. He had always expected to marry and have some of his own, but it had not happened yet. At thirty-nine years of age, he still hoped it would. In the meantime, he saw his nieces and nephews often and contented himself with that until one Sunday afternoon. He was working in his garden and two unlikely visitors arrived.

"Hey mister, what are you doing?" the little girl asked.

Luke looked up and saw two children staring wide-eyed in amazement at him and his garden. He smiled at the little girl and boy who had expressions that belied intense curiosity on their faces. "I'm doing my spring planting," he told them. He stood up, dusted himself off, and walked over to greet them. "See these?" he asked. He held out a handful of seeds. "These are Morning Glory. They're part of the Ipomaea family."

"What's that mean?" the little boy questioned.

"They're cousins of the potatoes."

"You got some potatoes?" the little boy asked.

Luke laughed. "Morning Glory are related to potatoes but their vines don't actually produce potatoes. By early summer, these seeds will turn into colorful flowering vines that are climbing all over these trellises."

"So you don't have potatoes?" the little girl said with a disappointed expression on her face.

"No," Luke replied, "but I do have milk and cookies." Both children immediately perked up in anticipation of the treat. Luke went inside to get the snack and came out a few minutes later with a plate of cookies, a carton of milk and some paper cups. The children were sitting on the ground inside the trellised area where he would soon be planting pumpkins. Luke walked over and sat down on the ground across from them. "I'm Luke," he told them.

"I'm Joanna and this is my little brother, Jimmy," the little girl replied.

"How did you happen to find me and my garden?" Luke asked.

"Easy," Jimmy answered. "We saw you over the fence."

"So, you're the ones who moved in next door a few weeks ago."

"Yup," Jimmy told him.

Luke watched as the children dived in and devoured the peanut butter cookies he had brought outside. He had piled close to half of a large package on a tray and was moderately surprised that Joanna and Jimmy managed to finish them all. He noted to himself that he'd have to get more next time he went to the store. He could see they really liked them.

✦ ✦ ✦

After their initial encounter with Luke, Joanna and Jimmy stopped over to see him almost daily. Jimmy would always ask, "Where are the potatoes?" The three of them would laugh and Luke would always serve something he knew the children liked.

Luke talked to Joanna and Jimmy about the pumpkin patch and invited them to help him plant it. They were delighted to get involved in the project. First, they created the pumpkin mounds. Luke showed them how tall and how wide the mounds needed to be. It took a whole weekend to get them ready, and when they were finished, there were seven mounds, each two feet high with a diameter of about five feet.

They planted enough seeds so that each mound might provide the germination place for at most five vines. Luke explained to them that pumpkins and their vines grew very fast. Once the seeds germinated, they would practically be able to sit and watch the vines grow—for it was not unusual for them to extend as much as an inch an hour.

"Will we be able to make pumpkin pie?" Jimmy asked.

"Probably not," Luke told him. "We may not get that

many pumpkins and most of the ones we do get won't get real big." Luke observed the expressions on the children's faces. They did not look happy.

"Can we grow something we can eat?" Joanna asked.

"Sure," Luke answered, wondering why it was so important to be able to eat what you grew. His enjoyment stemmed from the lush foliage and beautiful flowers. "We'll plant some yellow and green squash around the perimeter. Squash is real hearty and easy to grow."

Joanna and Jimmy smiled. "I've never had squash before," Joanna remarked.

"Can we take some home?" Jimmy piped in.

"Of course," Luke assured them.

✦ ✦ ✦

The magical pumpkin patch took on a life of it's own. Luke placed a fifty-five gallon drum at the entrance. He painted a sign on it that read, "No Potatoes Here." Together he and the children painted another sign, "Keep Out or Die!" which they staked to the side of the drum. On the other side of the trellises, which were now covered in exquisite Morning Glory varieties with pale blue, white and scarlet flowers, there was a small bench and two terrifying, life-size scarecrows.

Luke, Joanna, and Jimmy had had a wonderful time creating the scarecrows with clothes the children's mother donated for the project. The scarecrows were made with two pair of jeans, a couple of worn shirts and hats, an old pair of pantyhose, hangers and pieces of garden hose.

Together, they had stuffed the jeans and shirts with straw and affixed them to two large poles. The faces were made of nylons stuffed with straw. Luke ingeniously placed hanger wire at the elbows and knees of the scarecrows so the limbs could be bent. He also used hanger wire inside garden hose for the nose and eyes, which enabled him to give the figures some facial expression. The hats made the figures truly look like scarecrows.

Sometimes in the evening, the three of them would meet in their pumpkin patch hide-away, tell stories, and watch the pumpkin vines grow. Luke would always serve something to eat. They never complained when he served something nutritious instead of cookies or cake. They were very appreciative, which led him to believe that their parents had taught them good manners and provided well for their needs.

✦ ✦ ✦

Late in the summer, Luke suggested the children join him for a barbeque that evening. He said that he would get some hamburgers to grill and that they could cook a variety of vegetables from the garden. Joanna and Jimmy were delighted with the idea.

"Can we have hamburger buns, too?" Jimmy asked.

"Sure," Luke replied. "and I'll get ice cream for dessert."

"That would be very special," Joanna said brightly.

"Can we choose the flavors?" Jimmy asked.

Luke looked at them quizzically. They seemed more excited about ice cream than he would have expected. It made him think about how voraciously they ate cookies when he served them. Maybe their parents didn't serve sweets at home. He knew that some parents were very careful about the amount of sugar their children had. He hoped they would not be upset with him if they knew what their children were eating at his house.

Dinner was an event. Luke made everything on his grill. He wrapped the vegetables from the garden in aluminum foil. There were beans, and squash, which were seasoned with nasturtiums whose flowers and foliage tasted just like ground pepper. The hamburgers were cooked just perfectly and served in the buns Jimmy had requested. They drank fruit punch with the meal and topped things off with praline delight and chocolate marshmallow ice cream. It was a delightful evening. Luke enjoyed spending it with Joanna and Jimmy. He had grown very fond of them.

Luke wanted to send the leftovers home with the children for their parents. He carefully planned the menu so there would be more than enough. To his surprise, there was nothing left when they all stood to throw the paper plates and plastic utensils away. He realized that he had little idea of how much food growing children consumed.

"Thanks Luke," Joanna told him when it was time to go home for bed. "We had a wonderful time."

"It was a terrific dinner," Jimmy chimed in with a big grin on his face, "even if there weren't any potatoes."

✦ ✦ ✦

"May I help you?"

Luke looked up from this newspaper. A short middle-aged woman with a kind face peered down at him. She had permanent-curly hair that was thinning and an expression on her face that meant business. She clearly was not one of the food panty clients.

"I've seen you waiting out here for some time now." She smiled. "I wanted to make sure you didn't fall through the cracks. When it's this busy, we can sometimes overlook someone who needs attention."

Luke smiled. "Thanks for asking. I don't need any help. I'm just sitting here and waiting."

"My name is Marsha Willis," the woman told him as she extended her hand.

"Luke Simms," Luke countered, rising to his feet and extending his hand to meet hers.

"People don't usually come to God's Helping Hands to pass the time," Marsha told him.

"Yes, I realize that," Luke responded. "I came to help some neighbors."

"How's that?"

"A family moved in next door this past spring. The children come to visit often and have become my garden helpers. We have created a magical pumpkin patch surrounded by wild vines and extra tall sunflowers. We even have two unbelievable scarecrows that the kids helped me make. All summer long, I thought it was all the activities we were doing together that kept the kids coming back."

"It does sound wonderful."

"It is. And I am sure they have enjoyed it, but I finally realized that the activities were not the primary motivation for coming to visit and work in the garden."

"What do you mean?"

"Well, every time they came over, they were always asking what I had to eat. I never gave it much thought. But the last time they were over, their appetites seemed insatiable. I realized that they weren't getting enough to eat at home. That's when I took it upon myself to go over to their house and talk with their parents. It was just as I had suspected. There wasn't any food in the house. I was sorry it took me so long to figure it out."

"I think a lot of people don't realize that there is help available for people who need it," Marsha replied.

"I'd read about your pantry and shared the information. The parents were very interested but they weren't comfortable coming by themselves the first time. I told them I'd come with them."

Marsha smiled. "You did the right thing."

"What are neighbors for?" Luke replied, shrugging his shoulders as if to say it was nothing.

At that moment, he felt a child grab his arm. Before him stood Joanna and Jimmy. They were both full of energy and ready to help carry groceries to the car. Their parents were wheeling a cart full of staples that would help them get through the next month.

Marsha watched as Luke walked to the back door with the family he had brought in for support services. She just managed to hear the little girl proudly proclaim to her mother, "It's potatoes tonight, right? Can Luke stay for dinner?"

✦ ✦ ✦

CHAPTER
6

GOTCHA DAYS

✦ ✦ ✦

As a nation we are truly blessed to have so much. Why is it, then, you can go to any community and look into the eyes of a hungry child? Hunger is real and it is everywhere. So open your eyes and help!

William E. Kerr
President / CEO
Food Bank of Eastern Michigan

It was a crisp sunny spring day. The grass was greening up. The buds on the trees were starting to sprout leaves. And the sun was shining brightly on four young girls between the ages of ten and thirteen who were playing tag in the park. The littlest one, a fair skinned child with wispy long blond hair, struggled to keep up with the others.

Totally winded, she managed to reach out and touch one of the older girls, who had slowed down so she could be caught. "Gotcha," the little girl yelled out with satisfaction while trying to catch her breath. Her tall, stocky playmate with Mayan-like features and brick-colored skin put her arms around the smaller child and hugged her as they both panted and laughed.

When their breathing finally slowed, they looked up at the other two girls standing across the way. They had their hands on their hips with 'attitude' and were looking decidedly impatient. One was thin and muscular, and almost as tall as the girl who had just been caught. She had coffee-colored skin and curly black hair that fell to her shoulders in wonderful little ringlets. The other was an Asian child with straight dark hair that framed her face. She was rather slight but a very fast runner. "Betcha you can't catch me," she called out, baiting everyone else and the game was on again.

Some families celebrate birthdays in a big way. Others go all out for Christmas or Hanukkah. There are those who "pull out all the stops" for Halloween. And there are some who like to make very special plans for the Fourth of July. In the Wilson household, it was 'Gotcha Days' about which everyone got so excited. A 'Gotcha Day' was the anniversary of the day that you were chosen to become a member of the family. The Wilson children looked forward to other holidays, but 'Gotcha Days' were the best.

John met Lisa while he was in college. He was working toward his Bachelor of Science degree in education and student teaching in an area elementary school. John looked forward to teaching and had always hoped to meet a woman, who like him, had a desire to make the world a better place. When he met Lisa, he knew he had found the woman he wanted to marry. She was calm and thoughtful, as well as caring and concerned. She was also a teacher's aide who was working in the inner city helping children from disadvantaged backgrounds.

Unlike most young couples, John and Lisa Wilson decided to adopt children instead of birthing some of their own. A couple of years after they married, they made the decision to adopt a Native American infant. They named their first daughter Amanda. Two and a half years later, they adopted another baby who was from Korea. They called their second daughter, Elizabeth.

Parenthood came naturally to John and Lisa. They had always enjoyed working with children at school. Now they could experience the joy of having children of their own. Amanda and Elizabeth added new meaning to their lives, bringing a contentment they had never known before.

Years passed. John and Lisa, like other parents, struggled with their children as they progressed through different stages. They marveled at how the girls developed, how much they had to offer, and how affectionate they were. They sometimes became frustrated with the ongoing set of trials the girls skillfully managed to provide for them.

Amanda was ten and Elizabeth was seven. The Wilson household had a pleasant routine that was settled, comfortable and likely to remain so, or so they all thought.

✦ ✦ ✦

Several weeks earlier, a despondent woman in her mid 30s stopped in to see the executive director of a Kids Café in a nearby community. The woman had worn out her welcome at numerous food pantries in the community and was once again approaching Bound Together at All Saints Episcopal Church for a helping hand. She and her two daughters had been homeless seven times in as many years. They were living out of an old car, and it was taking its toll on the mother and her children.

The executive director, Reverend Barb, knew what to expect as soon as she saw her visitor. It had not been infrequent in the past for this family to need as much as half of their monthly resources from Bound Together. This was a significant drain on the agency's supplies, and while Reverend Barb knew she was not operating a pantry, she found it very difficult to turn away those who were in need.

"I'm giving my kids to you," the woman blurted out, taking Reverend Barb off guard. "I don't want the State to have 'em. And I don't want 'em to be split up."

Reverend Barb knew the woman had emotional problems but realized that she must have truly hit bottom to want to give up her children. She invited her into her office and tried to be as supportive as she could be.

"Are you sure you want to do this?" She paused for an answer, but the woman was unresponsive. "This is a major step you are suggesting. It will have a very big impact on the girls," she counseled. "Don't do something you might regret later." When the woman still did not answer, Reverend Barb spoke again. "Give it some more serious thought. Then come back to see me if this is really what you want to do. I will do my best to help you."

The woman returned the following day more anxious than she had been the day before. Her dress was untidy and her hair disheveled. She had a pained expression on her face. "I can't feed 'em. I can't afford 'em. Take 'em from me, please, and find 'em a good home."

✦ ✦ ✦

Reverend Barb had been given a mission. She had to find a family who would be willing to take temporary custody of ten-year-old Nicole and eight-year-old Michelle. She knew it would not be easy to place children as old as they were—especially those who had emotional problems stemming from an unstable home environment. She also had no idea how long the girls would actually need a place to live. Their mother's emotional health was so tenuous.

She approached countless families trying to find a suitable placement with little success. Some families offered to take one of the girls. Reverend Barb would not consider this out of respect to their mother's wishes and because she knew it would be best for them if they were not separated. Others responded by saying that they didn't have enough money to take care of their own kids and it would be unthinkable to consider having others to feed.

While she recognized the task before her was a formidable challenge, she knew in her heart that if she kept trying she would find a family to take the girls. And so it was when several weeks after she started her search, Reverend Barb found John and Lisa Wilson, a young couple who agreed to help out.

John and Lisa had a cramped, two-bedroom home. They didn't have a lot of money, but they had enough to meet their expenses. Their furniture wasn't elegant, but they had enough to feed and clothe their family. They didn't have a widescreen TV or high tech stereo equipment, but they had enough to contribute every week to a special fund, which was to be used to take Elizabeth to Korea so she could learn something about the land from which she came. Their home was rich with love. It was the kind of home Nicole and Michelle needed.

The Wilsons welcomed Nicole and Michelle with unbridled warmth. They treated the girls as though they were their own daughters. They worked hard with them since they had not been attending school regularly, and after a prolonged effort, were able to move them up to grade level. It was a struggle but there was definite improvement, which seemed to please Nicole and Michelle even more than it did John and Lisa. They started to feel better about themselves and have more confidence. They began to sense that they fit in.

John and Lisa hoped all the girls would become good friends. Amanda and Nicole were, after all, the same age; Elizabeth was only nine months older than Michelle.

It seemed logical that they would. But emotions are not logical, and young girls do not adapt as quickly as their parents would like when others try to infringe on what they feel is theirs. Amanda and Elizabeth weren't pleased about the prospect of sharing their bedroom, which had only one small closet. They weren't happy about sharing their parents, either.

Nicole and Michelle's natural mother by 'court order' was allowed supervised visitation. Reverend Barb was appointed to supervise. As it turned out, she made only one visit shortly after her daughters went to live with the Wilsons. She never asked to see them again.

What John and Lisa thought was going to be a temporary arrangement extended to a year and then two. This was complicated by the fact that while Amanda and Nicole eventually did start to warm up to each other, Elizabeth and Michelle did not. It seemed like they were constantly fighting as often with words as with fists. Michelle had more emotional problems than her big sister and had a difficult time getting along with everyone. It put a great strain on a household that was once calm and even.

"Reverend Barb," John called the woman who had come to be known around their home as the 'God' Grandmother because she took such a personal interest in the girls. "We are at our wit's end. We love Nicole and Michelle like our own. There isn't anything we wouldn't do for them. But Michelle continues to act out all the time. It's taking everything out of us and the other girls. I don't know how much longer we can continue to do this. We need a break to figure out how to proceed."

And then it was just the way it is in fairytales. Fairy 'God' Grandmother Barb waved her magic wand and said there was a place for Michelle in the summer camp program she ran. She would take her for a week, which would be fun for Michelle and a respite for everyone else in their household. John and Lisa breathed a sigh of relief.

Bound Together had been running a summer camp for a number of years. Initially, Reverend Barb had gathered funds to send ten children to a sleepover camp for a week. After a while, Reverend Barb realized this was not working as well as she had hoped. First, she was not able to send nearly as many children as she would have liked. Second, she discovered that children who were financially challenged often did not mix well with those from more affluent backgrounds. Fear and trust factors caused some of them to actually flunk out of summer camp and feel compelled to come home early.

As a result, she came to the conclusion that it made sense to rent an entire camp. This put her in the position to offer spaces to forty children for three days and two nights. It had been an overwhelming success. Children signed up months in advance for the opportunity to attend.

The only thing that saddened her was that there were long waiting lists. It was impossible to accommodate all the children who wanted to participate. While camp was already full, 'God' Grandmother Barb made arrangements to bring Michelle to summer camp with her.

Michelle felt very important having been selected as the only child in the Wilson household to get to go to camp with 'God' Grandmother Barb that summer. When she got there, she was overwhelmed with all the different things there were to do. Tetherball and basketball. Archery and swimming. Her favorite activity was the Gold Rush. This was a contest for which every camper was given a backpack. Every contestant was then sent out to search for as many gold rocks as they could find. The children used their backpacks to carry their gold rocks back to the flagpole where they were counted. The winner was the camper who collected the most gold rocks. All campers were entitled to keep their backpacks in return for the gold rocks they tendered.

'God' Grandmother Barb had to laugh the next morning when she entered the girls' dormitory. All the campers had actually slept with their backpacks. They wanted to make sure they didn't disappear overnight. Having a nice backpack was a new experience for all of these children. They were intent on taking their backpacks home when the camp experience was over.

Meanwhile, something unexpected happened back at the Wilson home. Elizabeth became hysterical. Much to her parents' surprise, she was upset that Michelle was away. In tears, she begged John and Lisa, "Bring my sister back." Elizabeth was afraid Michelle had been sent away for good. Even though she and Michelle were always fighting, she loved her big sister and wanted her to come home. When 'God' Grandmother Barb heard about this, she gave

Michelle another backpack to give to Elizabeth when she saw her. She hoped it would cement their relationship and get things off on a positive note upon her return.

The Wilsons could not afford to adopt Nicole and Michelle. With legal and court expenses, it would have cost them $4,000 each. Instead, permanent custody was arranged. The money the Wilsons would have had to spend for adoption was used to add a family room and an extra bedroom to their home. This provided desperately needed breathing space for everyone. It also symbolically sealed Nicole and Michelle's official new status in the family. A beautiful ceremony was held at their church to commemorate the permanent custody arrangement. It was a very special 'Gotcha Day.'

Every quarter, the Wilsons pile in their car and make a 'Cereal Run' to Bound Together. They always enjoy seeing 'God' Grandmother Barb. While there, they stock up on grits, turkey, ham, vegetables and other food items. They still don't have a lot of money, but they have enough to meet their expenses, even with two more children. They still have the same worn furniture and no wide screen TV, but they have enough to feed and clothe their family.

The Wilson home is one that is rich with love. The Wilsons provide everything their daughters need, but it helps to have added assistance from Bound Together. You might say the quarterly cereal run is a 'Gotcha Day.' It is a special time for them all to give thanks for the girls who were saved by God's kindness.

✦ ✦ ✦

PADRE ISLAND DAD

✦ ✦ ✦

When I was a child I remember a teacher asking the class what we had for breakfast. As a young immigrant child I was quite embarrassed to report that all I had was homemade bread and a glass of milk. I felt poor because most of the other children had boxed cereals or bacon & eggs, etc., which my family could not afford.

I was quickly given a reality check when she asked me to consider how fortunate I was to have anything at all to eat, let alone wonderful fresh bread made with loving hands.

Catherine Genovese
Owner
Candycane Christmas Tree Farm

Joey approached the Malaquite Beach Visitors Center. Every week he looked forward to Saturdays. That was when he would visit with Ranger Bob. Ranger Bob was a tall, well-built man in his late twenties who had graduated from college with a degree in natural resources a few years earlier. He had been delighted when he wrangled the job at Padre Island. Unlike many of his associates, Ranger Bob did not have to hold down two seasonal jobs. Padre Island National Park was open year round.

As Joey walked closer to the visitor center he realized that Ranger Bob was nowhere to be seen. He was sure it was after nine o'clock. That was the time when the Ranger appeared on Saturday mornings with trash bags to hand out to volunteers who arrived to help keep the island clean. It was part of the Texas Adopt-A-Beach program in which Joey participated. The look of anticipation on Joey's face quickly dissolved. Saturday would not be the same without

Ranger Bob. But then he saw the Ranger come from behind the visitor center with several new volunteers, and his spirits were restored.

Joey liked all the rangers, but Ranger Bob was special. He was the Ranger who months earlier had introduced Joey to the Junior Ranger program. Ranger Bob had given him a small booklet with information about the park's natural and human history. He'd instructed Joey to read the booklet and go to the exhibit area in the visitor center before trying to answer all the questions. Later, Ranger Bob had reviewed the test Joey completed on the seashore and environment.

When Joey passed with a perfect score, the Ranger had awarded him a certificate of completion and a plastic Junior Ranger badge that resembled his own. From that day forward, Joey felt a special bond with 'his' Ranger.

Ranger Bob made Joey feel important. He expressed a sincere interest in Joey and always engaged him in friendly banter. He asked Joey many questions and listened intently to what he had to say. Joey could always count on Ranger Bob to share interesting information about what was going on in the park. Joey looked up to Ranger Bob. He wanted to be just like him when he grew up.

"Hey there, Ranger Joey," the ranger called out. "How's it going? You gonna help me out today?" he asked, knowing full well that Joey always came to help him on Saturday.

"Of course I am," Joey responded. "We have to keep this island clean for all the visitors, don't we?" The Ranger realized that Joey was more familiar with the trash problem than many people because he spent so much time there.

Padre Island, the longest stretch of undeveloped barrier island in the world, has sixty-three miles of beautiful beach. However, the currents of the Gulf of Mexico perpetually bring unwanted debris from the Gulf to the northwest corner. While there is some litter recklessly cast away by thoughtless individuals, most of the trash comes from the fishing and shrimping industries, as well as from natural gas platforms.

Joey came up alongside Ranger Bob. He wished he had a uniform like Ranger Bob but remained content with his Junior Ranger badge, which he proudly pinned to his T-shirt every Saturday morning.

"Where're your dad and brother?" the Ranger asked. Ranger Bob asked Joey this question every Saturday and always got the same answer.

"Oh, they're down the beach doing other stuff. They're not interested in participating in the clean-up."

Ranger Bob wondered about Joey's dad but didn't want to pry. He figured one day, Joey would open up to him and tell him more about his family. Until then, he was content to listen and offer direction to the young boy who sought him out each week.

"I know you'd like to participate in the clean-up," Ranger Bob told Joey, "But there's something more exciting going on today that I'd like you to help me with."

"What's that?" Joey asked.

"I'm going to be joining some biologists who are here searching for sea turtle eggs. The biologists do this every spring. They take the eggs they find and bring them back to the park incubation facility."

"Yeah, I know about that. I was here last year when they released the turtles that were hatched back into the Gulf of Mexico. Why do they do that, anyway? Why not let them get there on their own?" Joey queried.

"You know, Joey, once that was the only way it happened, the way nature planned it. Unfortunately, the turtle population has decreased dramatically over the last century because people harvested the eggs and used turtles for food and consumer products. There are laws prohibiting these activities now, but the turtles need more than laws to protect them. We have five of the world's seven sea turtle species here in this area. And we don't want to see them become extinct. That's why we collect as many eggs as we can and take care of them. This way, they won't be preyed upon and eaten by animals."

Joey nodded his head. "There need to be laws to protect the turtles."

"So, would you like to go with me and the biologists for the search?"

"Sure," Joey agreed. He thought for a moment and then continued, "But can I still have an empty garbage bag before I leave?"

Joey was an enthusiastic worker who filled several trash bags every week when he helped with clean up. What had often perplexed the Ranger was that he always asked for an extra bag, which he never used. "Joey," the Ranger answered him, "you don't have to worry about the clean-up. Other people will do that. We're on an even more important mission today."

"Oh, I don't use the last bag for clean up," Joey told him.

"It doesn't look like rain," the Ranger laughed. Sometimes, he had seen tourists turn large trash bags upside down and make holes in them for their heads and arms. This was a resourceful way to deal with a sudden rain for which they were unprepared.

"I don't use it for rain, either," Joey told him. "It's for Dumpster diving."

"Dumpster diving?" the Ranger asked, incredulous that anyone would want to scavenge through Padre Island Dumpsters. "What ever could you expect to find here on the island?"

"You'd be surprised," Joey confided. "A lot of days visitors throw out some good stuff before they leave the park. They don't want to have to carry it home with them."

"Really?" the Ranger replied, not wanting to disrupt what Joey was telling him. "What kinds of things do you find? Beach chairs? Towels?"

Encouraged by the Ranger's interest, Joey proceeded. "Yeah. Sometimes, you find that kind of stuff. We do have a couple of chairs we found in Dumpsters that my dad repaired. But the best thing to find is food. You'd be surprised about the good food people throw away."

"What kind of food do you find?" Ranger Bob asked. Joey was revealing a side of his life he had never shared before. The Ranger liked Joey and was deeply concerned about what he was hearing.

"I find bags of chips or cookies," Joey shared. Sometimes, you can get lucky and find fried chicken or half-eaten hot dogs. It's not as good as the fish we catch, but sometimes there isn't a lot of fish to catch around here. The fishing is pretty good right now, though," Joey told his friend.

"Is it?" the Ranger interjected.

"Absolutely. There are a lot of trout and redfish. But my favorite is the mangrove snapper," Joey shared.

"Yeah, I like mangrove snapper, too," the Ranger agreed. "I haven't had any in a while, but it sure is tasty."

"We went fishing at South Beach last night and caught some for dinner," Joey volunteered. "Dad grilled it for me and Tommy."

"You're lucky your dad knows how to cook," the Ranger replied.

"Yeah. There's no one who can cook mangrove snapper over an open fire like my dad."

The Ranger knew Joey camped out often on the island with his dad and brother. He was beginning to wonder just how often.

"How often do you go fishing?" the Ranger asked.

"Oh, we fish every day," Joey told him. "How else are we gonna eat?"

"Is there fishing near where you live?" the Ranger queried.

Joey looked confused. "We live here on the island. I thought you knew that."

"No one lives here." Ranger Bob answered.

"We do," Joey replied. He had a very serious expression on his face.

The Ranger realized that he had stumbled onto some important information about the young boy who he had come to know over the last year. He did not want to offend him, but he did want to get more information. "I figured since there was only dry camping here, no hook ups or anything, that people would be discouraged from staying here for a long time," the Ranger answered. "You'd have to be pretty tough to weather this day in, day out."

"Oh, we are," Joey told him as he swelled his chest with pride. "We've got a great tent, and if it springs a leak, my dad just fixes it. I don't like the mosquitoes much, but we try to stay pretty close to the beach. The wind usually keeps them off the shore.

"Do you ever get a chance to shower?" the Ranger asked.

"Usually I just swim at the beach. That's what I like to do best. But sometimes, Dad and Tommy and me will use the bathrooms at the visitor center. People leave soap behind in the stalls."

"That's pretty convenient," Ranger Bob responded.

"Yeah," Joey agreed.

That afternoon, Joey went with Ranger Bob and the biologists in search of turtle eggs. It was a lot of work, and

Joey discovered that turtle eggs were not as easy to find as trash. Still, they did have some success. Joey even managed to find some eggs when he went exploring on his own. He was thrilled with his find, and all the adults showered praise on him. Joey was a young man who had a genuine love of the outdoors, and participating in the turtle egg rescue was one more exciting experience for him.

At the end of the day, Ranger Bob gave Joey a large garbage bag. "Thanks for your help, Ranger Joey. You were a very valuable member of the team today."

Joey beamed. Saturday was his favorite day of the week and this Saturday had been especially exciting. He and Ranger Bob shook hands. "See you next week," he told the Ranger.

"See ya," Ranger Bob smiled and gave Joey a pat on the back as he headed away from the visitor center.

✦ ✦ ✦

The following Saturday morning, Ranger Bob was at his usual post. He arrived at work just before nine o'clock, changed into his uniform and went out in front of the visitor center with an armful of trash bags. Many volunteers straggled in over the course of the morning to get bags from him and search for debris along the shoreline of the island. It was like every other Saturday for him except for one thing. Ranger Joey was not there to talk with him.

Ranger Bob missed the lively conversation he and Joey always shared. He thought about Joey's enthusiasm and zest for life, and considered the endless barrage of questions Joey always asked in his search to learn more about his surroundings. Not having kids yet himself, the Ranger missed the way Joey always looked up to him and wanted his advice. Ranger Bob felt a sense of loss deep inside. He wondered if he and Joey would ever have any of their special conversations again and figured it was unlikely. Even if they did meet again, things would not be the same. Joey probably thought that Ranger Bob had betrayed him. But Ranger Bob was confident he had done the right thing.

Over and over, Ranger Bob reviewed the conversation he had had with Joey a week earlier. Joey had been living on Padre Island with his dad and brother for as long as he could remember. Neither he nor his brother was enrolled in school. The clothes they wore and the food they ate came primarily from their Dumpster finds. The Ranger knew that this was not the way for a young boy to grow.

The Monday after their last meeting, the Ranger had called Child Protective Services. The agency sent out a couple of representatives who asked the Ranger to locate the campsite where Joey lived with his brother and dad. It had taken a while to find it, but there were clues everywhere that pointed the Ranger in the right direction.

It was early evening when the threesome arrived at the site. The two men who were wearing suits and wingtip shoes were ill prepared for the hike. They were sweating profusely and swearing at the hungry mosquitoes that persisted in feasting on them. Their shoes and pant cuffs were covered in marshy sand. They wondered how they had been chosen for this ordeal and looked forward to getting back to Corpus Christi.

Joey's dad heard them first as they approached the tent. He stepped out to speak with the men and told the boys to stay inside.

"What can I do for you?" Joey's father asked.
One of the men showed some identification. "We're here to talk with you about your sons, Mr...." There was a long pause. The man had expected Joey's father to tell him his last name. "Your name, sir?"

"Fred Lang," he answered defensively.

"Mr. Lang, we understand you have two children living here with you."

"Yeah," he replied. "That'd be my sons, Joey and Tommy. You have a problem with that?"

"Mr. Lang, let's make this as easy as possible," the other man spoke. "We're here as representatives from the

State of Texas. The State of Texas has laws to protect those who cannot protect themselves."

The first man spoke again, clearly making a reference to information the Ranger had provided. "There need to be laws to protect the children just like there need to be laws to protect the turtles."

Joey must have heard him and drawn a connection to the conversation he'd had with Ranger Bob. Ignoring his father's directions, he peeked his head outside of the tent. He looked up at the men talking to his father and then glanced around and saw Ranger Bob. The expression in his eyes was a mixture of hurt and anger. He had shared his deepest secrets with the Ranger, who he thought was his friend, and the Ranger had betrayed him.

Joey and his brother were taken into protective custody and were to be placed in foster homes—homes with running water and food that came from the refrigerator. They would have clean clothes to wear and regular classes to attend. They would be looked after by responsible adults who might grow to love them, but not people who could ever love them like their dad.

Parental love, however, means providing ample shelter and food, medicine and clothing. Some folks need a helping hand—especially little rangers!

✦ ✦ ✦

8

SOCIAL SECURITY BLUES

✦ ✦ ✦

In my opinion, lack of education due to hunger, has contributed to crime in our society. Hunger exists in Oakland County, Michigan, one of the wealthiest counties in the United States. Step up to the plate. Make a difference. Help us feed our young people. Today!

Ed Bahoura
President/Owner
Save-A-Lot Food Stores
Pontiac & Madison Heights, MI

"We'll be in the house less than twenty minutes," Crystal assured her daughter. "The kids can stay in the car."

"Are you sure it will be O.K.?" Brianna asked tentatively.

"Do you wanna have a replay of yesterday?" the mother barked. "I'm not chasin' your kids around that house again. And I don't think they'll want us back if we have the kids with us."

Brianna's shoulders dropped in resignation as she buckled under her mother's protests. She, too, expected they wouldn't be gone long. Leaving the kids alone would have to be all right. She and her mother got out of their 1989 Chevy and slammed the front doors of the car behind them. Crystal started to cross the street. "Aren't you gonna lock the doors?" Brianna asked her mother.

"You growed up just fine," her mother answered, glaring back at her.

Brianna looked at her children. The baby and five-year-old were crying. The seven-year-old had his hands, nose and lips pressed against the windowpane. The sorrowful expression on his face challenged her to stay behind with him. She shrugged her head, turned and followed her mother into the gray frame house across the street while trying to repress the image of her unhappy children in the car.

Crystal rang the bell, but no one answered. She knocked persistently, but still there was no reply. She started to fidget while she stood waiting, swaying as she transferred her weight from one leg to the other. If she didn't get her 'fix' it was going to be a long, torturous night. She started to bang on the door with both fists.

"Hold on. Hold on." A black man in his early 30s leisurely approached the door, unfastened the bolt and slowly pulled the door open. "A little impatient, aren't we?" he asked with a knowing grin.

"You got somethin' we want," Crystal railed.

"I know," he replied, the grin on his face broadening. "Come on in."

The man closed and bolted the door once they entered. He gestured to the time-worn couches in the living room as if to say, "You know the routine." He then wandered into a back room for what seemed like forever to Crystal. "You got the money with you?" he called out to them.

"We got money," Crystal yelled back, feeling decidedly impatient. She motioned to Brianna to take the

$20 bill from her wallet. "How 'bout you gettin' them rocks out here?"

"You'll like this new stuff I just got in," he told them upon his return. His voice was soothing and seductive. "It's better than anything I've had in a long time." He held out the two crack rocks, which were the color of white sand. Crystal grabbed the $20 bill from Brianna and thrust it at the man.

"Now Crystal, you know better than that. That's only enough for one of you."

"Give it to Brianna," she demanded hoarsely. Brianna looked at her mother tentatively. "Go on," her mother ordered. "Take it."

Brianna took the rock in her hand. The man then handed her the rod of what remained of a cheap pen. A piece of metal scouring pad was stuffed into it at one end. Brianna crumbled up the crack rock and pressed it into the metal. She picked up the matchbox on the coffee table in front of her and pulled out a match to light the makeshift pipe.

When the crack ignited, she took a drag from the other end. In less than fifteen seconds, Brianna was feeling the effects. It didn't matter anymore that her mother wasn't getting any. She no longer cared that her kids were alone outside in an unlocked car. She had no thought of the future or the despair of not knowing from where the money for tomorrow's fix would come. Nothing mattered but the ultimate rush she felt streaming though her body.

"You done?" the mother asked in a demanding tone once Brianna finished the smoke. Brianna didn't answer.

She was oblivious to her mother's demeaning tone. "Get on outside to those kids of yours," Crystal ordered.

"But what about you, Mama?" Brianna naively queried.

"Don't you worry about me. I'll be outside soon."

Brianna got up to leave. The man who had supplied her with the crack followed her to the door and let her out. Once outside, she looked around and then focused on the car across the street. She walked over and climbed inside. Her children were overheated. She realized they were hollering loudly enough to attract the attention of a passing police car. "Who cares," she thought to herself. Brianna felt good. She felt real good. She rolled her window down part way to cool the car off and waited for her mother to join her. She was surprised but not bothered when twenty-five minutes passed before Crystal returned.

"It sure took you long enough to get out here," Brianna reprimanded Crystal in a tone she never would have used if she hadn't been high. "What took you so long?"

"It's all good," her mother answered enigmatically. She put her car key in the ignition, waited for the engine to turn over and pulled out into the street. The tires screeched as Crystal slammed her foot down on the accelerator. Anyone would have thought she was drunk.

✦ ✦ ✦

Althea and Jake Johnson married when she was seventeen and he was twenty. They had been married for forty-eight reasonably contented years and in that time had never left the state of Michigan. Jake had worked as a handyman until he had a stroke a few years earlier. That, and his diabetes, now left him confined to a wheelchair. Althea worked for thirty-seven years in a local clothing store whose losses during the last recession had caused it to go out of business. She now stayed home and looked after her husband. They were happy in their retirement.

The Johnsons owned their own home free and clear, a cozy two-bedroom house in Pontiac. It was clean, neat and comfortable. They were frugal and managed to live on the social security checks they both received. All totaled, that was eight hundred dollars a month. While it was barely enough, especially with the two hundred dollar monthly contribution they made toward Jake's medicine, they were thankful for what they had and for the supplemental benefits Medicaid provided which made it possible to pay for Jake's pills. It was good that they had worked hard and spent their money wisely when they were young. Having no car or house payments made life financially doable.

Althea bent over and lovingly kissed her husband. "The baby is sleeping in the crib," she stoically reassured him, "and I'll be home before the other kids get back from school." Neither of them alluded to the appointment she had made for later that afternoon. They had a great deal of anxiety about their situation but didn't see the point of discussing it any further.

Moments later, Jake heard the door close behind his wife. He wheeled himself over to the TV, turned it on and tuned in to watch one of his favorite afternoon shows. He hoped the baby would stay asleep until his wife returned.

Once on the porch, Althea glanced at the car in the driveway but decided to walk to Lighthouse, the local agency that provided emergency food. "It's such a pretty day," she thought. "I can use the exercise and it will save on gas." She held onto the railing as she walked down the porch steps and proceeded on the sidewalk in the direction of the agency.

Althea was a strong woman, emotionally healthy and physically robust. She had had the energy and perseverance to hold down a job, manage a household, and raise both a daughter and a granddaughter. She and Jake were active in their church and had always contributed their time and efforts to help others. Everyone looked to them as upstanding citizens. Friends and neighbors shook their heads sadly behind their backs and wondered why bad things happened to good people.

The caseworker at Lighthouse looked up as Althea entered her office. "Good afternoon, Mrs. Johnson. Please come in and take a seat."

"Thank you." Althea replied. "I appreciate your responding so quickly to my call." Althea sat down, took off her coat and pushed the shoulders of the coat arms onto the chair behind her. She was wearing a freshly pressed, shirtwaist dress and her hair was tied back conservatively in a bun. The caseworker figured she must be in her middle sixties.

"I'm Linda," the caseworker introduced herself. "How can we help you here at Lighthouse, Mrs. Johnson?" Tears welled up in Althea's eyes. The words she wanted to speak choked in her throat. "Take your time," the caseworker responded sensitively to her visitor's discomfort.

Althea didn't know where to start. "My husband and I aren't as young as we once were," she shared. "We don't have the energy we used to have. I don't think the girls understand." Linda nodded her head sympathetically. "They used to drop the kids off for an overnight every once in a while and then I'd take them to school. I love it when the kids come to visit," she paused. "But last week, they dropped off the great-grandbabies and they never came back."

"I'm not sure I understand," Linda replied. "Who are the girls?"

"The girls are my daughter, Crystal, and my granddaughter, her daughter, Brianna. Brianna has three children." Althea continued without coming up for air. "My husband is in a wheelchair, Linda. He can't even leave the house without my help. We barely make ends meet as it is. How are we going to feed our great-grandchildren?"

"Don't Crystal and Brianna understand they can't put this on you and your husband?" Linda asked, placing the responsibility squarely where it belonged.

Althea's body stiffened. She was a proud woman, and it was not easy for her to come and ask for help. She regained her composure and sat up straight in her chair. "Linda," she paused, "Crystal and Brianna are crack addicts."

Linda was immediately startled. She had seen repeatedly how drugs could destroy a family. It was not unusual for grandparents to have childrearing responsibilities thrust upon them when they ought to have been able to relax and enjoy their twilight years. But great-grandparents? Her heart went out to the woman who was sitting in front of her. Althea and Jake had a formidable task in front of them. Lighthouse could help, but it couldn't make the problem go away.

"We can help you, Mrs. Johnson," Linda consoled her. You and your husband have had a great burden cast upon you. But we can help ease it." Althea smiled. Linda seemed to know what she was talking about. Perhaps she and Jake could get through this.

Linda pulled out a drawer in the filing cabinet next to her desk and started to select different forms. "We'll arrange for temporary custody. We'll fill out the Family Independence Agency forms so you can get a bridge card to help feed the children."

"What's a bridge card?" Mrs. Johnson asked.

"It's what's replaced food stamps."

"Oh, Linda, you're an angel sent from Heaven."

Linda smiled. "Mrs. Johnson, I'm not an angel. I just know how to get you the assistance you need. We'll arrange to get Social Security income for the children, and help from the state with the children's medical expenses."

"Can you do that?" Althea asked in amazement.

"Yes, we can," Linda replied. "Are the children enrolled in school?"

"Oh yes," Mrs. Johnson replied with pride. "They even take the bus. It drops them off right in front of our home."

"See," Linda reassured her. "You hardly need my help." Instead of responding positively to her comment, Mrs. Johnson started to look worried again. "What's wrong?" Linda asked.

"I can't wait for the bridge card," Mrs. Johnson confided. "I don't have enough to feed the children now. Jake and I don't eat very much. I think that's how we manage to get by on as little as we do. But growing children...."

"It's O.K. We have an emergency food supply here. We'll send you home with enough food today to make sure your great-grandbabies don't go hungry. We'll set you up so you can come back here every thirty days and we'll give you additional food to supplement the relief you get with the bridge card." Althea started to look more relaxed and heaved a sigh of relief.

✦ ✦ ✦

That evening, Althea and Jake sat around the dining room table with their great-grandchildren. Althea had prepared a healthy dinner where all the food groups were represented. She had roasted chicken because she knew it was her eldest great grandson's favorite. Althea had smiled as she washed potatoes for baking. She knew how much her other great grandson liked to cut them open and mash them with lots of margarine. The baby loved corn so Althea had made creamed corn for her, thinking that because she would feed it to her on a spoon, it would be one thing that didn't get thrown on the floor. All the children had milk.

For dessert, Althea made an apple cobbler. Althea's apple cobbler was always a special treat. When she was younger, she had often made it for church potluck dinners. When she didn't, her friends were disappointed. This ensured she would make it the next time there was an opportunity. Althea had learned how to prepare apple cobbler from her mother. For that reason, making this dessert was not only special for those who enjoyed her baking, it was special for her. It made her feel warm inside to share it with those for whom she cared. It also gave her a connection to an earlier period in her life that was more carefree.

"Is this a holiday?" her oldest great-grandson asked, looking up from his meal with a big smile on his face.

"I don't think we've had such a good meal since last Thanksgiving," his younger brother chimed in between bites.

"More," the baby said enthusiastically, as she tossed a piece of chicken on the floor.

Althea and Jake looked at each other and smiled. It had been a long time since they had been able to sit down to a full meal like the one before them. Only that morning, they had worried about how they were going to provide for their great-grandchildren. Now, with the help of Lighthouse, they were confident that they could manage.

"Pass the chicken," one of the boys asked.

"Hey, that's the last piece," the other called out, trying to stab it.

"Grandma Althea," the first whined.

"Why don't you split it?" she suggested while bending over to cut it in half with her knife. "There will always be enough to go around if we are considerate of one another and share."

✦ ✦ ✦

A Good Deed Is Never Lost

+ + +

The hunger situation in this nation is truly our most frightening domestic problem. The raw statistics are bad enough...almost a million people right here in Michigan in need of some sort of government food assistance... the rolls of the hungry grew an astonishing 64% just over the past year... close to half of all those in need are children. But then, as if the data weren't awful enough, you read the stories of families who, merely because of unforeseen circumstances, like divorce, or loss of job, or inability of the bread winner to maintain work, suddenly find themselves in dire need of food. We cannot abide the perilous predicament of hunger faced by so many of our fellow citizens and their families. Simply put, it is the personal responsibility of all of us to do everything possible to aid those in our community who suffer hunger. Any effort less than that is completely unacceptable.

Joe Berwanger
Vice President/General Manager
WDIV-TV
Detroit, MI

Rosa slowly approached the maternity ward nursing station. While she had been to the hospital years earlier, she had never ventured further than the emergency room before. Somehow she felt surprised by all the stainless steel and stark white paint everywhere. It was at once pristine and antiseptic. All the staff seemed so busy, scurrying around in white hospital uniforms, intent on their tasks although it was not clear to her just what they were. At the station no one appeared to notice her. She felt out of place and wondered how Juanita had experienced this decidedly foreign environment. Finally, an attendant looked up. "May I help you?"

"I'm here to visit Juanita Sanchez," Rosa told her, showing the pass she had received in the main lobby.

The attendant glanced at her chart. "That'll be room 338A," she replied, smiling. Noticing the bewildered expression on Rosa's face, she stood up to show her the way.

"It's just around the corner," she remarked, leading Rosa to the room. Once there, she knocked on the door, which was opened only a crack and peeked in. "You have company!"

The girl in the bed smiled widely when she saw Rosa. A few months shy of sixteen, she had signed herself into the hospital the night before. She wished she had thought to call Rosa in the throws of the labor pains, but it had not occurred to her until the morning.

Rosa looked at Juanita. She was so thin. Her eyes were sunken and her hair was uncombed, but there was a luminous glow about her.

"Oh, Rosa. I knew you come," Juanita cheerfully greeted her in broken English. Rosa smiled and went over to Juanita's bedside. "I want to call you sooner but it all happen too quick," Juanita continued. "It was all I could do to get here for myself. And *gracias a Dios*, the labor was short." She laughed softly and gestured to the infant, carefully wrapped in clean, white hospital blankets who was sleeping at her side. "She is beautiful, no?"

Tears welled up in Rosa's eyes because the baby was beautiful, but also because she was worried about Juanita. Rosa knew that having a baby was one of the special blessings of life. She had a child of her own. But Juanita was hardly more than a child herself. She was too young to have the responsibilities of motherhood.

Still, Rosa understood well how such things happened, since she had once been rebellious herself. She, like Juanita, had felt trapped in her parents' home. Unlike Juanita, she had

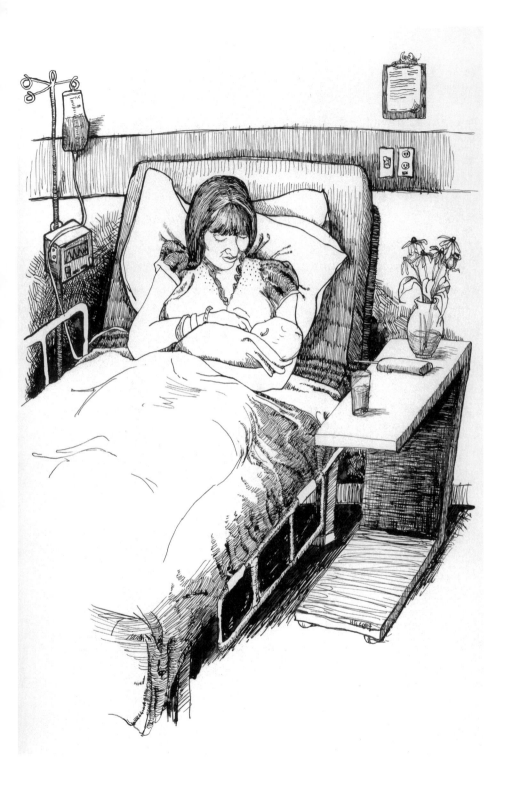

not become pregnant. She had found other ways to rebel.

Juanita had seen pregnancy and the birth of her child as a way out. The child's father was the son of illegal immigrants. A year older than Juanita, he had promised to take her as his bride and rescue her from her home situation. His plan went awry when his parents had decided to move to another city in the hope of finding better jobs. Too young to be on his own, he went along with them. He had promised Juanita he would send for her when the baby was born. He wrote only once, and she never heard from him again. When the baby arrived, she found herself alone with no one upon whom she could lean.

Two months earlier, her parents had been rounded up in an immigration sweep at the factory where they worked. The authorities demanded to know where their children were because they wanted to send them back to Mexico with their parents. Under pressure, Juanita's mother and father shared the names of all their children— except Juanita. They knew her due date was coming soon and wanted their new grandchild to be a genuine American citizen. They would not let Juanita be deported with them. A friend of the family had been dispatched to the apartment so Juanita would not be there when representatives from immigration arrived.

Rosa had great empathy for Juanita and the situation in which she found herself. She was thankful she had not gotten pregnant before she married. She had had an ugly scrape with an uncle who had tried to molest her on a family visit out of town when she was eleven, but she had told her parents about it and they were careful she would never be left alone with him again.

Rosa thought back to when she was fifteen. Like Juanita, she was part of a large Mexican family whose parents spent countless hours away from home in an effort to provide for their children. Both she and Juanita, as the eldest daughters in a Mexican family, had to manage the household and take care of their younger siblings. Neither was mature enough to deal with the pressure and rebelled.

Rosa started searching for a gang to join when she was only seven. She had desperately needed to be with a group of young people who were there for each other— a group that would give her the sense of family she did not receive at home.

Unexpectedly, she found herself an outcast even in gang circles. Having grown up in a family that was for-the-most-part Americanized, her English was very good and her Spanish very poor. The Mexicans ostracized her because she was not Mexican enough for them. The blacks and Asians called her a 'wigger' and accused her of trying to act like she was one of them. By the age of ten, Rosa started smoking and drinking. There was rarely any food in the house. While her parents were away, she would search the house for alcohol and consume it all, which would often leave her in a stupor. *Estomago hambriento no escucha rezones.* There is no arguing with an empty stomach.

Rosa ran away from home when she was fifteen, in an effort to escape responsibilities that had been cast

upon her years before she was ready for them. She had
had assurances from her friends that she could stay at their
houses, but their parents were not so welcoming. She would
sometimes shower and eat at her friends' homes, but when
nightfall came, she was on her own. She shook her head as
she thought about how she had dropped out of high school
when she needed only one more credit to graduate. She was
glad she had had the sense to get her G.E.D.

✦ ✦ ✦

"Her name is Esperanza," Juanita said, looking from
the baby to Rosa.

Rosa realized that her mind had wandered.
"Esperanza, that's a pretty name."

"Yes," Juanita agreed. "I discuss it with the priest. I
tell him I want a name that has special meaning. The priest
tell me that Esperanza means hope. I believe there is hope,
Rosa. Esperanza is my hope for a future that is bright.
Together, we embark on a better life."

"I believe you are right, Juanita. There was hope
before she arrived - but now, now there is Esperanza!" The
two young women laughed with joy in anticipation of all the
possibilities their young lives suggested, possibilities that
could only be limited by their dreams.

Rosa had met Juanita four months earlier at her
community youth center. At twenty-three years of age,
Rosa had been written up and interviewed repeatedly in the

local media. She was a 'Mother Theresa' sort who selflessly worked to improve the lives of young people.

It had started when she was seventeen. She had found herself surrounded by young people who were floundering - just as she had been. Many came from homes where their parents were rarely around. Few of them were getting enough to eat, and they did not have the financial resources to buy food. They felt unloved and lacked a sense of direction.

Rosa started helping through gang outreach, going directly to the kids wherever they were. She'd talk with them, play pool with them, and encourage them to be productive. A friend who had a reception hall offered her its use on Sundays. Delighted to have use of the facility, Rosa started a program for twenty-four young people.

She waitressed at the hall other days and spent all of her earnings on art supplies and food for Sunday programs. After one month of operation, close to two hundred youngsters between the ages of twelve and nineteen were coming to participate. Word spread quickly, with early participants bringing friends and siblings to get involved. Rosa was encouraged because whites and blacks, Hispanics and Burmese would all sit around together—eating, meeting, talking and interacting with one another.

One day several months after Rosa started her Sunday program, she visited a high school in the neighborhood where she was doing outreach and saw a 'For Rent' sign on a vacant building across the street. She decided it was a sign from God and took down the phone number to call and find out the rent.

The landlord was so impressed with Rosa and what she was doing that she offered her the building rent-free for three months. Rosa was overjoyed. Later that day though, the landlord called to say she had changed her mind. After careful consideration, she had decided to give the building outright to Rosa.

In the early days, Rosa did not know about grants or food banks or 501c3 status. Her work came directly from the heart, and her funds came directly from her meager earnings and the contributions she was able to get from area businesses. As her operation grew, she began to write grants and obtain money in that manner. She even did grant development for other organizations. They would compensate her by letting the young people in her programs take advantage of their facilities.

By the time Rosa was twenty-two, she was married with a child, but this did not inhibit her desire to grow. Her organization had an annual budget in excess of $300,000 a year and she was feeding close to four hundred children twice a day. She never took a salary because she wanted all the money to go toward helping young people in the area.

Sometimes she would frequent a local soup kitchen to satisfy her own needs for nourishment. It was an irony of life that she was, on the one hand, a local celebrity, widely interviewed and appearing on TV - and on the other hand, lining up with the needy in the community for food.

Rosa was helping many teens who desperately needed the food, nurturing, and lessons she offered. Juanita's brothers started attending her programs daily. They would come home and tell Juanita about Rosa's center. Their eyes sparkled as they talked about the hearty meals. They brought home watercolor drawings and ink paintings they made there, and Juanita would proudly tape their artwork on the walls and the refrigerator. She secretly wished that she were a boy, so she too could participate. Still, Juanita was happy for them.

It took some persuading on their part, but the boys finally got Juanita to visit the center with them. She was surprised on her first visit to discover the center was actually coed. The boys immediately introduced Juanita to Rosa.

When Rosa first met Juanita, she was surprised by how thin she was. Rosa knew the signs of malnutrition, and it was clear to her that Juanita was not getting enough to eat. Rosa would have been concerned about this under any circumstances, but she was particularly troubled because Juanita's protruding belly exposed a secret. She was pregnant.

"Won't you have something to eat?" Rosa offered.

"Oh no," Juanita had replied. "I just come to help out."

Although it was clear she was hungry, Juanita would not allow herself to accept anything that was offered to her. She felt it would be rude. Rosa understood the Mexican culture and realized that she would have to make numerous overtures before Juanita would be willing to break bread at the center. She counted on Juanita returning with her brothers so this would happen.

Rosa was pleased when Juanita came again the following day. Once more Rosa invited her to sit down and eat. Again Juanita insisted she had only come to help. When Juanita visited the center the third day, she finally accepted Rosa's offer of a hot meal.- but only if she could help clean up afterward.

Juanita sat down and slowly ate the tuna casserole and green beans that were placed before her. When she was done, she looked up with a smile on her face. It felt good to have a full belly. "So now I will help," she declared looking directly at Rosa.

"This is good," Rosa told her. "You accept my hospitality and then extend hospitality to others."

"*A' quien te da el capon, dale la pierna e el alon*," Juanita replied.

"What does that mean?" Rosa asked.

"To him who gives the capon, give the leg and the wing," Juanita replied.

"Ah," Rosa answered. "We say,'one good turn deserves another.'"

"Yes, that's it," Juanita agreed.

And so it was that Juanita began to come to the center every day with her brothers. Over time, she started to gain some weight and began to look healthier. Rosa took a special interest in Juanita. She made sure Juanita received milk to drink every day. She wanted to get her medical care but it was an impossibility. To represent Juanita, she needed a release form from her parents. To get the release form, she had to talk with them.

Rosa tried repeatedly to contact Juanita's parents, but she had no success. Rosa assumed they were frightened and believed she was trying to trap them. As a last resort, Rosa approached organizations that had a "Don't ask, don't tell" policy. Through these organizations, she was able to get vitamins for Juanita and limited medical care.

✦ ✦ ✦

"When will you be released?" Rosa asked, her thoughts coming around to the young woman in the bed.

"The hospitals don't keep me here very long," Juanita replied. "I be leaving tomorrow."

"What can I do to help you?" Rosa responded.

"Oh, Rosa, you do so much already," Juanita sighed. "It is up to me now."

"And what are your plans?"

"I have to go home - back to Mexico," Juanita shared. "My family, it needs me."

"I understand," Rosa nodded.

"And I need them," Juanita told her, demonstrating her recently gained wisdom.

"You are right," Rosa agreed. "But please remember that you are always welcome here. I need good helpers, and I have discovered that my best helpers are those I have helped." She smiled.

"In Spanish, we say, '*El hacer bien nunca se pierd*,'" Juanita told her. "It mean a good deed is never lost."

"Yes," Rosa replied. "A good deed is never lost. Many of the people I have helped go on to help others. Some come back to volunteer at the center. It is very gratifying to see helping others become a way of life."

"I help," Juanita responded, "in Mexico."

"Yes," Rosa replied, "But right now, it is little Esperanza who needs your help." Rosa pulled a small, gift-wrapped box out her purse and handed it to Juanita. "Here's a little something for Esperanza."

Juanita carefully unwrapped the gift. She removed the lid from the box and pushed back the cotton. Inside was a tiny black velvet jewelry bag with a small drawstring. She loosened the strings and pulled out the silver pendant inside. It was a miniature religious medal of Our Lady of Guadalupe, the Patron Saint of Mexico and the Americas. *"Que medallitas de la Virgencita mas Linda!"* Juanita exclaimed. "I never forget you. And your good deeds is never lost on me."

✦ ✦ ✦

CHAPTER
10

MOTHER OF THE NIGHT

✦ ✦ ✦

As I was growing up, the two things I could always be sure of was plenty to eat and lively mealtimes with my family. My heart breaks when I think of how many Vermont children don't know that sense of safety and security.

Deborah Flateman
Chief Executive Officer
Vermont Foodbank

Jessica always looked forward to Saturdays. That was the day her grandma and grandpa would come over to take her on an all day outing. Sometimes, they would go to the park together. Other times, they would take her to the beach. Once they took her to a produce market that stretched for blocks. Many of the street vendors had told her how pretty she was. She liked that. Some of them had given her a sample taste of the honey rock melons or Georgia nectarines they were selling.

Some of the foods she tried she had never tasted before. One vendor, who was selling hand-dipped chocolates, offered her a piece. She had tentatively looked up at her grandmother for approval since the candy was not wrapped. Her grandmother had given the necessary nod and Jessica had been delighted to receive the gift. By the time she finished it she had dark chocolate and caramel all over her face and hands. It had been fun to lick it off her fingers.

She and her grandparents had finally left the market mid-afternoon when most of the stalls were closing down. They had been able to purchase food to take home with them at a very cheap price because the people selling it did not want to take it back to their farms with them.

The last Saturday Jessica's grandparents picked her up from the apartment, they took her on a picnic. Then they all went to see an old Three Stooges movie at the public library. There were many parents and grandparents there with small children like her. Everyone laughed during the movie because so many funny things happened. Jessica had a great time.

It had been a wonderful day until they returned home.

Grandma had started fighting with Jessica's mother. They were yelling at each other so loud that Jessica had to cover her ears. When it was over, Grandma had taken a couple of large boxes into Jessica's bedroom and filled them with her clothing and toys. Jessica had gone back to her grandparents' house that night and had been living with them ever since. She didn't know exactly how long ago that was, but it had been summertime. Now there was snow on the ground.

✦ ✦ ✦

Jessica knew it was nighttime. Her mother had put her to bed hours earlier after a short bedtime story. Usually she slept through the night, but this night was different. At first she thought she was dreaming. But then she realized she was awake and that there were loud sounds coming from the next room. She could not discern what the sounds were, but she knew they frightened her. She felt a sense of alarm pass over her and a corresponding tightening feeling in her chest. She was sure that someone was trying to hurt her mother.

Jessica wondered what she could do. She knew she was little and wished that somehow she could stop the fight in the next room. She thought about calling her grandmother who always seemed to be able to take care of everything, but she didn't know how to use the telephone yet. She saw herself carefully sneaking out of her room, then quietly making her way to the front door in an effort to get help. But she knew that she probably couldn't get the door open all by herself. She had just learned to open the doors in the apartment. The front door was much heavier and difficult to use.

Her mother was screaming and she heard the unfamiliar voice of a man. It wasn't her grandfather. His voice was always calm and soothing. And it wasn't the voice of any of the men her mother said hello to when they went on walks in the neighborhood. This was a man she did not know. She wondered what he was doing here and why he was hurting her mother.

Jessica thought of hiding in her closet. It would be safe there. Instead, she bravely tumbled out of bed and quietly toddled over to her mother's room. The door was slightly ajar, so she was able to peer in to see what was happening. The man was in bed with her mother. He was on top of her and she appeared to be wrestling with him. Neither of them had on any clothes. Jessica was transfixed by what she was observing and just when she thought she could no longer stop herself from screaming, the struggling and loud noises stopped.

Jessica was confused. She continued to stand there and watch the stillness. Not long after the noises stopped, the man and her mother got up and dressed. They did not appear to be angry with one another. "You're real good, Missy," she heard the man tell her mother. "Real good." Jessica was even more confused now. Her mother's name was not 'Missy.' Jessica turned and toddled back to her room. She sensed that now was not the time to question her mother about what she had just seen. She wondered if there would ever be a good time to ask for an explanation.

The next morning, Jessica's mother threw on her terry robe. After loosely belting it, she looked at herself in the mirror and smiled. The night was behind her. It was going to be a good day. She wandered into Jessica's bedroom to help her dress. Jessica looked closely at her mother. She seemed happy. There didn't seem to be any bruises on her body.

Her mother announced that the two of them were going to take a walk to the supermarket. "I got lots of money for groceries," she told Jessica. "You can pick out a special treat for yourself while we're there." Jessica knew she should have felt happy. There wasn't always enough money for groceries, and there was rarely enough for her to get a special treat. Curiously, she only felt tired and unhappy.

Jessica and her mother spent the day together. They went grocery shopping and bought more food than Jessica had seen in a long time. Her mother pushed her up and down the aisles in a grocery cart and let her choose all the things she wanted including Lucky Charms and chocolate milk. They even brought strawberry ice cream home, which was her favorite food, and sandwich cookies with cream filling.

In the afternoon, they went to the park, where Jessica played with friends by the slide and swings while her mother visited with other mothers who had small children. Jessica was happy because she was doing all the things she liked to do. She was also happy because her mother appeared to be having a good time.

That night, her mother read her a short bedtime story as usual and tucked her in bed. She kissed Jessica goodnight and wished her pleasant dreams. Jessica fell asleep quickly. But once again, she awoke when it was still dark. Just like the previous night, she heard loud sounds coming from her mother's bedroom. The sounds frightened her just has they had the night before, but she courageously slid out of bed to see what was happening.

The door to her mother's room was open, so she had a clear view of what was happening. Again she saw her mother naked and in bed with a strange man. This time he was black. She was sure her mother was struggling to get free, but Jessica could see that the man was bigger and stronger than her mother so she could not escape.

When the fighting stopped, they both got up and dressed. Jessica saw the man take some papers out of his wallet and hand it to her mother. She folded them in half and slid them inside her nightstand drawer.

Like the previous night, Jessica toddled back to her room unseen. She didn't know what to think or say. She considered asking her grandma about it on their next outing.

✦ ✦ ✦

Jessica was happy living with her grandparents. They rented a small, two-bedroom house so she had her own room just like at the apartment. Her grandparents kept mostly breakfast foods in the house, cereal and milk, and sometimes eggs. Once in a while, they would surprise her with a special snack. For lunch and dinner, they almost always went to a soup kitchen nearby. Jessica didn't realize it, but they were living on a fixed income and depended on the soup kitchen for the nourishment they needed.

Jessica liked going to the soup kitchen. It reminded her of when she used to go out with her mother to a restaurant. There were some differences, however. At the soup kitchen, you didn't order what you wanted, you got what everyone else was having. Also, there were a lot more people at the soup kitchen than any restaurant to which she had ever been with her mother. She asked her grandmother how many people there were, and her grandmother laughed and told her sometimes as many as two hundred people. Jessica enjoyed the attention many of her grandparents' friends showered on her, but she was disappointed there weren't many children her age there.

While some people did not help out, many who came to eat would help clean up after meals. The soup kitchen was like a second home to them. They would stack chairs and wipe down the tables. Some would clear dishes and help wash them. One man took on the task of mopping the front hallway and cleaning the bathrooms. The people who helped out showed their appreciation this way. They might not have had the money they needed for food, but they could maintain their dignity by 'paying' with the service they provided.

For several weeks before Christmas, Jessica heard everyone at the soup kitchen talking about the big Christmas dinner that was planned. Jessica didn't remember her last Christmas very well because she had been only two, but her excitement for the holiday grew every day as she heard her grandparents and others talk about it.

There was to be a grand meal with turkey and ham, sweet potatoes, cranberry sauce, green beans and something she heard people refer to as stuffing. She didn't know what stuffing was, but it was something you ate with turkey, which everyone appeared to enjoy. She wanted to try it. For dessert, the director had said there would be all kinds of pies. A lot of people traditionally donated pies to the soup kitchen over the Christmas holidays. Jessica's favorite pie was pumpkin, and she was assured she could have as big a piece as she wanted. There'd even be whipped cream.

Christmas Day finally came. She and her grandparents put on their best clothes for the holiday celebration. Her grandmother put on her green velvet dress, which Jessica had only seen her wear once before when they had gone to a special service at church. Her grandfather wore his black suit with a tie that had Santa Claus on it. He laughed when Jessica told him she wanted to sit on his lap and tell him what she wanted for Christmas. He told her to wait until they got to the party, so she could ask the real Santa.

Jessica had one special party dress, which her grandmother had brought home for her several weeks earlier after a visit to a local thrift shop. The dress was pink with a white sash and ruffles. It had a fluffy slip sewn into the skirt that Jessica thought was very special. She wanted to put on makeup like her grandmother but was told she was too young. Her grandmother did share a couple drops of cologne with her, which she dabbed on her granddaughter's neck below her ears. Jessica felt very grown up.

Jessica and her grandparents bundled up and headed to the party. Not only would there be a festive meal, but some carolers were going to come and sing. Also, Jessica had heard that the children who attended always received a gift. Like all children, Jessica liked presents. She hoped she would get one of the dolls she had seen on TV.

Once inside the facility, Grandpa took his wife's coat and that of little Jessica. After hanging them up, the threesome proceeded to join the merry gathering. The room was decorated with silver and gold garlands of tinsel and English Holly intertwined with Ivy. There was a large Douglas Fir on the far side of the room that volunteers had put up and decorated several weeks earlier.

Several of her grandparents' friends approached and offered them eggnog. They 'ooed' and 'ahed' over Jessica. She was a pretty child anyway, but today, she looked particularly nice. Her grandmother had curled her shoulder length blond hair and tied it back with a ribbon that set off her pale blue eyes. Her party dress was very special and necessarily called everyone's attention to her.

Jessica saw Santa sitting on the other side of the room. There was a long line of children waiting to sit on his lap to tell him what they wanted for Christmas. Each child spent several minutes with Santa, explaining how important it was that they receive a certain item. This year, the outreach coordinator had been unable to find anyone to play Santa, so she had donned the traditional beard and red suit so the children would not be disappointed.

Santa knew that while she could not fulfill all their special requests, there was a large stash of wrapped gifts in the back room, which were sure to please every child in attendance. The soup kitchen had received overflow from a children's agency in the area, as well as monetary donations from other sources, which were used to buy items that young people traditionally asked for like soccer balls, dolls and learning games.

Jessica climbed up on Santa's lamp. "And don't you look pretty," Santa told her.

"Thank you, Santa," Jessica answered, thinking that the director must be the real Santa because she looked just like the pictures she'd seen. "You look very jolly."

"Ho, ho, ho," Santa replied in a voice that was an octave higher than was customarily expected from the Christmas icon. "And what do you want for Christmas?" Santa asked.

Jessica thought for a moment. "I want my mommy," she told Santa. The director was stumped. All the other children had asked for gifts that could be purchased in a store. Getting a child's mommy was more than Santa could promise. She began to carefully craft her answer but before she could speak, Jessica jumped up and hugged her. "Oh Santa," she screamed, "You're the best." The director was confused and surprised by Jessica's animated response, especially when the child jumped off her lap before she had even responded to her request.

Jessica, who had not seen her mother in months, now saw her standing near the entrance of the room. She was talking with her grandparents and everyone was smiling.

Jessica eagerly ran over to join them.

Her mother bent down and hugged her. It reminded her how much she had missed her mother's hugs. She felt tears in her eyes and couldn't understand why she felt like crying. Jessica raised her hands to her eyes to brush the tears away and surprised herself when she unexpectedly started to laugh. Her mother laughed, too.

Jessica loved her grandparents but she had never really understood why she had had to leave home and live with them. She was glad no one was angry any more. She didn't know what had changed but she had a feeling that everything was back to normal.

+ + +

About The Author

Dr. Carol Dunitz is a speaker, writer, producer and consultant. Her colorful presentations for which she dresses in costume include Schmooze or Lose, Interpersonal Communication in the Workplace, Top Notch Customer Service, and Sure Fire Sales and Negotiating. She has written and produced numerous audio CDs to supplement her programs that teach audiences how to communicate more effectively.

Carol Dunitz is also a seasoned marketing professional who provides comprehensive communication services to business. She creates advertising campaigns that deliver formidable results by developing strategies and implementing them through high-powered writing and graphics. Among other things, Dunitz writes executive speeches, scripts, promotional literature, and web sites. She is noted for her ability to make anything interesting and easy-to-understand.

Dunitz is also the author of *Louder Than Thunder*.

Dr. Dunitz has a B.A. in Theatre and English
from the University of Michigan and a Ph.D. in Speech
Communication and Theatre from Wayne State University.

About The Illustrator

Helen Gotlib is a prolific printmaker who works in lithography, intaglio and wood block mediums. Her printmaking and illustrations are highly imaginative and demonstrate a strong interest in exploring form and fantasy. She has traveled extensively in Japan, China and Israel. Her observations of people and customs across the globe have influenced her perception of the human body and how expressive it is.

Helen Gotlib received her B.F.A. from the University of Michigan School of Art and Design. She is the recipient of numerous art awards.

Winners of Food Bank of Oakland County
"Put a Face on Hunger" Contest

Miles Hudson; Samantha Acton; Fiona D'Agostino;
Anne Marie Brinkman; Robert Clemente; Lee Cleaveland;
Sydney Ann Hirsh; Erick Lin; Brian Baylor; Anna Way;
Daniel Kelly Wu

Sidney Ann Hirsh

Lee Cleaveland

Anna Way

Fiona D'Agostino

Brian Baylor

Miles Hudson

Anne Marie Brinkman

Daniel Kelly Wu

hungry

Not hungry

What
a
difference
it
Makes

Robert Clemente

Erick Lin

Samantha Acton